THE REAL STORY
UNDERSTANDING THE
BIG PICTURE OF THE BIBLE

EDWARD SRI & CURTIS MARTIN

It is our hope and prayer that this book will open the Scriptures to you and that you will encounter Jesus Christ by the frequent reading of the sacred texts.

"Lectio divina": the diligent reading of Sacred Scripture accompanied by prayer brings about that intimate dialogue in which the person reading hears God who is speaking, and in praying, responds to him with trusting openness of heart. If it is effectively promoted, this practice will bring to the Church -- I am convinced of it -- a new spiritual springtime.

-Pope Benedict XVI

Nihil obstat: Benjamin Akers, STL
                  Censor Librorum

Imprimatur: +Most Reverend Samuel J Aquila, STL
                Archbishop of Denver

Published by Beacon Publishing
in agreement with EPIC Publishing,
a subsidiary of FOCUS
www.focusonline.org

ISBN: 978-1-937509-54-5

Dynamic Catholic® and Be Bold. Be Catholic.®
are registered trademarks of The Dynamic Catholic Institute.

For more information on this title
and other books and CDs available through
the Dynamic Catholic Book Program,
please visit: DynamicCatholic.com

The Dynamic Catholic Institute

2200 Arbor Tech Drive

Hebron, KY 41048

Phone 1–859–980–7900

Email info@DynamicCatholic.com

Printed in the United States of America.

With gratitude to
Scott Hahn
Teacher, Mentor and Friend

Edward Sri & Curtis Martin

Table of Contents

INTRODUCTION
DISCOVERING THE REAL STORY OF THE BIBLE

The Bible can be intimidating. After all, it is no ordinary book; it's more like a library. It consists of 73 books, written in different languages, by different authors, and to diverse audiences at various periods of time. It also contains many different *kinds* of writings: law, poetry, letters, history, and prophecy, to name a few. And while some people might be familiar with the major stories of the Bible—Noah and the flood, Moses and the Exodus, David and Goliath, Jesus and the cross—few understand how all these varied stories actually fit together.

In this short work, you will discover the "big picture" of the Bible—how the many smaller stories of Scripture fit into the overarching story of God's covenant family plan, centered on the person and mission of Jesus Christ. As the *Catechism of the Catholic Church* explains, "Different as the books which comprise it may be, Scripture is a unity by reason of the unity of God's plan, of which Christ Jesus is the center and heart" (CCC 112).

We will break down that larger narrative into concise, easy-to-read chapters that focus on key characters and events in the drama of salvation—from Adam, Noah, and Abraham to Moses, David, and Daniel. But we will always do so with the "big picture" in mind. At every step of the way, we will see how God is preparing His people for the coming of Jesus Christ and the Church He established. Special attention will be given to the first book of the Bible, the Book of Genesis, which introduces the main characters, plot, family lines and promises that shape the rest of the salvation history. With this foundation in mind, the unity of God's plan as revealed in the Bible will shine out more clearly.

We hope that this book will help readers see the Bible not as a random collection of stories about people, places, and events from long ago, but as an epic saga about God's infinite love for us, the struggle between good and evil in the world, and the crucial role we each are called to play as we enter this drama with our own lives. That in the end, is the *real* story of Scripture.

CHAPTER ONE
TROUBLE IN PARADISE
The Call and Fall of Adam
(Genesis 1-3)

Don't be fooled: There's a lot more going on in the opening chapter of the Bible than you might expect. But to grasp its powerful meaning, you must be willing to see the story from the perspective of its original audience: the ancient Israelites.

The way ancient near-eastern cultures like Israel told stories and passed on their history is very different from our own. They did not typically offer straightforward, chronological, "play-by-play" accounts, as modern-day historians or newspaper reporters might do. Instead, the Biblical writers often organized material by themes and employed elaborate literary techniques that involved repetition, parallelism, allusion, and alliteration—artistry that readers today often miss.

This is certainly the case with the first chapter of the Bible, Genesis 1. The account of the six days of creation, the divine commands ("Let there be light!"), and God's rest on the seventh day was never intended to be read like a scientific textbook. Rather, the passage uses figurative language and poetic devices to communicate its beautiful message about creation and God's plan for the human family. These rich theological points in

Genesis 1 are more deeply appreciated when we consider the way the six days of creation unfold in the narrative.

Numerous scholars have pointed out that there is a connection in the narrative between the first three days and the next three days of creation. On the first three days, God creates day and night (first day), sky and sea (second day), and land and vegetation (third day). Then, on the fourth day, God creates the sun, moon, and stars to rule over the day and night, corresponding to what He created on the first day. On the fifth day, God creates the birds to fill the sky and the fish to fill the sea, corresponding to the second day. And on the sixth day, God creates the beasts that crawl on the earth, corresponding to the land created on the third day.

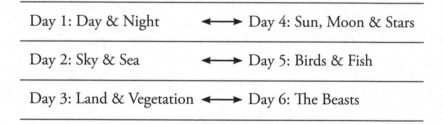

Day 1: Day & Night ⟷ Day 4: Sun, Moon & Stars

Day 2: Sky & Sea ⟷ Day 5: Birds & Fish

Day 3: Land & Vegetation ⟷ Day 6: The Beasts

The author of Genesis 1 is underscoring a series of parallels between the first and last three days of creation to reveal God as the divine architect, creating the universe with great order. He first creates three realms on days 1-3 (time, space, and life), and then He creates the rulers over those realms in days 4-6 (sun, moon, and stars over time; birds and fish filling sky and sea; and the beasts over the land). Finally, God creates man and woman as the crowning of His creation, making them in His image and likeness, and giving them the mission to rule over all creation: "Let them have dominion over the fish of the sea, and over the birds of the air, and over the cattle, and over all the earth" (Gn 1:26). All this is missed if we do not take into account the literary artistry of the biblical writers.

A Subversive Message

Much is also missed if we fail to consider the historical context in which this account was written. Other ancient near-eastern cultures around Israel had their own stories about how the world came into existence and how human beings were created. But Israel's story stands out for its emphasis on monotheism—the belief in only one God.

The pagan nations around Israel believed in multiple deities, many of whom were associated with the things of this world. They worshipped the sun, moon, and stars; the sea monsters were powerful deities, and other pagan gods were associated with the images of various animals.

For Genesis 1, therefore, to proclaim that Israel's God is the one true God who created the sun, moon, stars, sea creatures, and all the animals would have been a countercultural and subversive message. Genesis would be highlighting how the very gods that the pagans worship are actually not deities at all, but merely creatures of Israel's God, the one and only true God!

Image Is Everything

The drama of Genesis 1 next moves from the cosmic perspective of God's creating the sun, moon, and stars to the climactic moment when God finally creates man: "Then God said, 'Let us make man in our image, after our likeness.'" (Gn 1:26)

Christians often talk about how we are made in the "image of God." But what does this really *mean*?

While this concept has many layers of theological meaning (see CCC 356-357), what would have stood out to the ancient Israelites hearing the story of creation is that Adam and Eve have a relationship with God that is truly extraordinary. Nothing else in the visible world even comes close to the intimate communion God establishes with Adam and Eve.

In the Bible, being made in the *image* of someone else implies a father-and-son relationship. In fact, the next time this word is used in Genesis, it describes the relationship between Adam and his own son, Seth: Adam "became the father of a son in his own likeness, after his image, and named him Seth" (Gn 5:3).

If Seth is in the image of his father Adam, what would that tell us about Adam's being made in the image of God? Adam is being revealed as God's son. Thus, the entire narrative of the Bible begins with an astonishing truth about our identity: We are not mere creatures of the Creator or servants of an almighty deity. We are called to an intimate relationship with this infinite God as His children, made in His image.

The Fatherhood of God

This passage also gives us a glimpse of who *God* is. If Genesis 1 highlights how Adam was created as God's son, this would suggest that God is meant to be understood not just as Lord but also as *Father*.

The rest of Genesis 1 and 2 goes on to show God's fatherly care for Adam. God provides Adam with a garden full of water to drink and fruits and vegetation to eat. He creates the animals and allows Adam to name them and care for them, showing Adam his mission to rule over and care for all of God's natural creation. He even provides Adam with a partner: his bride, Eve.

In the midst of the story, God gives Adam only one restrictive law, a single "Thou shall not": He says to Adam, "You may freely eat of every tree of the garden; but of the tree of the knowledge of good and evil you shall not eat, for in the day that you eat of it you shall die" (Gn 2:16-17). This leads us to a crucial question for understanding the story of Adam, as well as the story of our own lives: Why does God give the law?

God does not give this law to Adam in order to control him and restrict his freedom. In fact, God's words underscore the broad liberty He was giving Adam to eat *freely* from *every* other tree in the garden. There is only one tree from which God does not want Adam to eat: the tree of knowledge of good and evil.

Neither is the law given merely to test Adam's obedience. There is a much deeper purpose to the command. The text says God warns Adam about this one tree because He does not want Adam to be harmed: "*for in the day that you eat of it you shall die.*" In other words, God gives this law to protect Adam from some danger that is symbolized by the tree of knowledge of good and evil (*cf.* CCC 396).[1] Here, we can begin to see how the moral law flows from God's love for us. As Pope John Paul II once explained: "God, who alone is good, knows perfectly what is good for man, and by virtue of his very love, proposes this good to man in the commandments."[2]

The Instruction Manual

Think of God's moral law as an instruction manual for our lives. When purchasing a car, one receives an owner's manual that explains how best to operate the vehicle. The manufacturer who made the car knows how it works and gives us operating instructions to ensure that the car functions properly. No one views these instructions as impositions on our lives. They are not given to control us or restrict our freedom; they are given to help us use the vehicle well.

Similarly, the moral law is like God's instruction manual for our lives. God is the divine manufacturer: He made us and knows how we work. He knows that certain actions will lead us to happiness, while other acts will end only in frustration and emptiness. That's why God gives the moral law—to help guide us on the pathway to happiness.

The Serpent's Strategy: Rules vs. Relationship

The law flows from the Father's heart. But the devil wants Adam and Eve (and all of us) to view God's law *apart* from His love— to see the command merely as a rule, not as an expression of his relationship with us.

Consider the serpent's first words to Eve: "Did God say, 'You shall not eat of any tree of the garden'?" (Gn 3:1). Here, the serpent simply refers to the Lord as "God" (in Hebrew, the word is *Elohim*). This title is used in Genesis 1 to describe God as the Creator of the universe. The serpent's use of this title here is particularly striking, because the rest of Genesis 2-3 characteristically refers to God as "the Lord God" (in Hebrew, *Yahweh Elohim*), which elsewhere in the Bible expresses God's intimacy with His people as Israel's covenant partner. In Genesis 2, it is the "Lord God" who creates man from the ground and breathes life into him, who creates the animals and allows Adam to name them, and who creates the woman from Adam's side. Indeed, the "Lord God" is a loving God, intimately involved in Adam's and Eve's lives, providing for them as His children.

But the serpent will have none of this. He does not call God *Yahweh Elohim.* He wants Eve to think of God as a remote deity, a distant creator—one who gives a burdensome law. It is as if the serpent is saying, "Did that distant Creator, that powerful lawgiver, say, 'You shall not eat of *any* trees of the garden'?" The serpent wants them to think of God as an oppressive lawgiver whose rule limits their freedom.

The woman responds by mentioning that they may eat from other trees, but that if they eat from the tree in the midst of the garden, they would die (Gn 3:2-3). To this, the serpent says: "You will not die. For God knows that when you eat of it your eyes will be opened, and you will be like God, knowing good and evil" (Gn 3:4).

Attack on God's Fatherhood

Feel the gravity of the serpent's words: In saying, "You will *not* die," the serpent is calling God a liar. According to the serpent, the tree is *not* harmful; it is actually something that will make them become like God, who is so afraid of their eating from the tree and becoming like Him that He makes up this law in order to keep them under His control.

Notice that the devil is not simply trying to get Adam and Eve to break a rule; ultimately, he is trying to get them to break a relationship. The first sin, then, involves questioning God's fatherly goodness. As the Catechism explains, "Man, tempted by the devil, let his trust in his Creator die in his heart and, abusing his freedom, disobeyed God's command. This is what man's first sin consisted of. All subsequent sin would be disobedience toward God and lack of trust in his goodness" (CCC 397).

The first temptation, and every one since, involves an attack on God's loving Fatherhood. In our own relativistic world, many people adopt the serpent's view about God's moral law: They doubt that there really is a moral law that is given for our good.

When a culture views religion as "just a bunch of rules," and morality as the Church "trying to tell others what to do with their lives," it no longer sees the moral law as coming from the heart of a loving Father who wants what is best for us. Like Adam and Eve, our modern world has not just abandoned moral truth; it has bought into the serpent's lie about God Himself.

The 'First Gospel'

Through sin, Adam and Eve bring discord into the original harmony they had with God and find themselves in desperate need of being restored. Spiritually separated from God and having introduced death into the world, Adam and Eve now have a problem that they are incapable of solving on their own. Right at this desperate moment, God offers a message of hope.

After the Fall, God confronts the serpent, saying, "I will put enmity between you and the woman, and between your seed and her seed; he shall bruise your head, and you shall bruise his heel" (Gn 3:15). These words represent the first time in the Bible when God's plan of salvation is prophetically foreshadowed. The imagery of the strife between the serpent's offspring and the woman's offspring depicts a long battle between those who will follow the serpent's ways and those descendants of the woman who will follow God's ways. In the end, however, the woman is described as having a descendant who will defeat the devil. Since the use of the imagery of *crushing the head* in the Bible denotes a king defeating his enemies, this passage portrays the woman as having a royal offspring who will emerge to defeat the serpent.

Christians have called this passage the *Protoevangelium,* or the "first Gospel." According to the Catechism, these words represent the first prophecy about the redemptive work of Christ:

> The Christian tradition sees in this passage an announcement of the "New Adam" who, because he "became obedient unto death, even death on a cross," makes amends superabundantly for the disobedience of Adam. Furthermore, many…have seen the woman announced in the *Protoevangelium* as Mary, the mother of Christ, the "new Eve." (CCC 411)

The New Adam

But Genesis 3 not only provides a prophecy about Christ's victory over the devil; the narrative also foreshadows *how* Jesus will restore the sons of Adam to covenant with God.

Consider what happened after Adam was tested in the Garden of Eden and ate of the tree of knowledge of good and evil. As a result of the fall, Adam faces several curses. His work will not be as easy as it once was in the Garden of Eden; now, he will have to "sweat" in his labors (Gn 3:19) while his crops bear "thorns and thistles" (Gn 3:18). Even the ground where he will work is cursed (Gn 3:17). The most severe of the curses, however, is that he will no longer live forever but return to the ground from which he was made. God says to Adam, "You are dust, and to dust you shall return" (Gn 3:19).

All this sheds light on the climax of Christ's mission in His passion and death. As the New Adam, Jesus confronts the curses laid on Adam that have plagued the human family ever since the Fall. Like Adam, Jesus, on the night before He died, enters a garden—the Garden of Gethsemane—where He is tested (Mt 26:36-46). There, He takes on Adam's sweat as He experiences sweat-like drops of blood falling from His face. On Good Friday, Jesus symbolically takes on the curse of Adam's thorns as He is handed over to the Roman soldiers, who place a crown of thorns on His head (Mt 27:29). Finally, Jesus even takes on the curse of Adam's death as He goes to a tree—the wood of the cross—and dies on Calvary. And, like Adam, Jesus is placed in the cursed ground, where He is buried in a tomb. It is precisely from the darkness of that tomb in the cursed ground that Jesus, the Light of the World, rises victoriously from the dead on Easter Sunday to shine the light of salvation at the dawn of the new creation.[3]

CHAPTER TWO
A NEW CREATION
Noah and the Flood
(Genesis 4-9)

Our tour through the Bible now takes us into the Scripture's first two genealogies. Admittedly, for modern readers, a genealogy seems to be just a long list of names—probably not that important, and certainly not that interesting. As Biblical scholar N. T. Wright put it, "Reading other people's genealogies is about as exciting as watching other people's holiday videos."[4]

But for the ancient Israelites, a genealogy was more than just a long list of names. Each name told a story and underscored key twists and turns in Israel's history. The reader who skips the genealogies will often miss out on crucial points God wants to make in the overarching narrative of the Bible.

This is certainly the case with the Bible's first two genealogies, which trace the descendants of two of Adam's sons, Cain and Seth.

A Tale of Two Cities

The first genealogy chronicles Cain's descendants and illustrates how one man's sin ripples through the generations (Gn 4:17-24).

After murdering his brother Abel, Cain turns his back on God and breaks fellowship with his family (Gn 4:16). The account of Cain's sin is immediately followed by a list of his descendants, in which we see men and women raising up children who do not know the Lord and whose decisions bear evidence of an ever-increasing breakdown in family life and morality. The genealogy shows how the descendants of Cain are known for polygamy, vengeance, violence, murder, and pride, as they name a city after themselves (Gn 4:19-24).

Unlike Cain, however, Adam and Eve continue to seek the Lord. They are blessed with another son, Seth. As a family, they begin to "call upon the name of the Lord"—a Biblical phrase associated with worship (see Gn 12:8, 13:4, and 26:25; Ps 80:18-19 and 105:1). In contrast with Cain's descendants, who build up their own name (Gn 4:16), Seth's family focuses on God's name in worship. The birth of Seth heralds a second genealogy in Genesis 5. Here we see how this faithful son of Adam and Eve also fathers a family, but his descendants manifest notably different qualities from the disgraced offspring of Cain.

Notice the stark contrasts. Seth's family worships the one true God (Gn 4:26), whereas Cain's line has turned away from the Lord (Gn 4:16). Seth's line lives in God's blessing (Gn 5:2), whereas Cain's family lives under a curse (Gn 4:11). Seth's family calls on the name of the Lord and seeks to give glory to God (Gn 4:26), whereas Cain's family seeks to give glory to its members, naming cities after its own children (Gn. 4:17). Seth's family is characterized by the son in the seventh generation, Enoch, who "walked with God" (Gn 5:22-24); whereas Cain's line is exemplified by the son of the sixth generation, Lamech, who lives a life of polygamy and violence (Gn 4:19-24).

Seth's line	Cain's line
• Lives in God's blessing (Gn 5:2)	• Lives in God's curse (Gn 4:11)
• His family "calls upon the *name* of the Lord" and gives glory to God (Gn 4:17) (Emphasis added)	• His family *names* a city after itself and turns away from the Lord (Gn 4:16) (Emphasis added)
• Worships the one true God (Gn 4:26) and walks with God (Gn 5:22-24)	• Family characterized by acts of polygamy, vengeance, violence, murder, and pride as it names a city after itself (Gn 4:17-23)

These two genealogies illustrate two fundamentally different types of cultures: One is characterized by a pursuit of God, the other by a pursuit of one's own selfish desires. Although centuries have passed, individual lives, families, and cultures are still defined by this essential question: What is our first love? It is a question each of us must ask himself: Is my heart first and foremost truly seeking God and His plan for my life? Or is it running more after the pleasures, honors, luxuries, and entertainments of this world? Seth's family sought the Lord, calling on His name and striving to walk in His ways. But Cain's family put itself first and became distracted by worldly glory, sexual pleasure, and making a name for itself.

Thousands of years after Cain and Seth, we face a similar choice. As St. Augustine described in his classic work *The City of God,* the contrasts between the line of Seth and the line of Cain continue right up to the present era—between those who live in what he called "the city of God" and those who reject Him and choose to live in "the city of man":

We see then that the two cities were created by two kinds of love: the earthly city was created by self-love reaching the point of contempt for God, the Heavenly City by the love of God carried as far as contempt of self. In fact, the earthly city glories in itself, the Heavenly City glories in the Lord. The former looks for glory from men, the latter finds its highest glory in God, the witness of a good conscience. The earthly lifts up its head in its own glory, the Heavenly City says to its God, "My glory; you lift up my head." In the former, the lust for domination lords it over its princes as over the nations it subjugates; in the other both those put in authority and those subject to them serve one another in love.[5]

St. Augustine's description of the two cities challenges us to examine our own lives: What is truly first in your heart? What city will you help build up?

Why the Flood?

So, if there were at least one righteous group of people—the line of Seth—on the earth, why did God send a flood that punished the *whole* human family?

Our first clue is found at the start of the Bible's account of the flood, which notes that "the sons of God saw that the daughters of men were fair; and they took to wife such of them as they chose" (Gn 6:2). Immediately after this, God indicates His displeasure and announces that He plans to punish the whole of humanity: "My spirit shall not abide in man for ever, for he is flesh, but his days shall be a hundred and twenty years" (Gn 6:3).

What led God to this conclusion? In order to answer this question, we must take a deeper look at the context and ask, "Who were the sons of God? Who were the daughters of men? And why would God be opposed to their marrying?"

Whenever we encounter a statement in Scripture that appears unclear, the first place we should look for clarification is the immediate context. In the two chapters that immediately precede this scene, we learned of two genealogies that tell a story of two families with radically different values and lifestyles. Genesis 4 focuses on Cain's family, which is centered on man and has turned its back on God. Chapter five focuses on Seth's family, which calls on the Lord's name and walks with God. But in Genesis 6, "the sons of God" married "the daughters of men," and, as a result, God punished the human family with a flood (Gn 6:1-7).

In light of these two genealogies, Genesis 6:1 begins to make more sense. The "sons of God" would refer to the godly family of Seth, and the "daughters of men" would refer to the disgraced descendants of Cain.⁶ The text thus seems to indicate that the sons of God in the Sethite line were attracted to ungodly women from the Cainite line and married them. As the once faithful line of Seth is undermined by the introduction of godless spouses, the covenant family is weakened and God is grieved. The whole earth now has become corrupt, and God sends the flood.

This intermarriage between the faithful and the unfaithful introduces an oft-repeated theme within the Scriptures: that when God's people intermarry with the pagans, they also turn toward the pagan gods and immoral lifestyle (see Nm 25:1-3, 1 Kgs 11:1-8). This is the context for understanding the flood.

A New Creation

The presentation of the flood in Genesis 6-9 echoes the account of creation in Genesis 1. In establishing this parallel, the author of Genesis is trying to highlight the fact that sin is bringing about a *reversal* of creation. In other words, the beautiful order and harmony that God established in the world has been distorted because of sin. We see this borne out in the way the flood account begins by noting how "God saw the earth, and behold, it was corrupt" (Gn 6:12). This simple statement stands in dramatic contrast with what God saw at the climax of the creation week in Genesis 1: "God saw everything that he had made, and behold, it was very good" (Gn 1:31). But now, sin has taken its toll, and God's good creation has been disfigured.

Similarly, notice what the Bible actually says about how the flood came about. Many of us may think of the flood as a rainstorm that lasted a long time, but the Scriptures present something far more catastrophic. At the beginning of creation, a watery chaos known as the *tehom* in Hebrew (meaning "the deep") covered the earth (Gn 7:11). God's spirit hovered over the waters, separating them to create the sky and the sea, and then taming them to bring forth the land that would serve as a suitable home for humanity.

In the flood, these separated waters come crashing back together, and the watery chaos is unleashed. "The fountains of the great deep [*tehom*] burst forth, and the windows of the heavens were opened" (Gn 7:11). This was not simply a prolonged downpour; the language seems to indicate a deluge of water coming from every direction. The chaotic waters of the sea would be swelling over the land, while the waters of the sky would be collapsing upon them. In the flood, God's creation is devastated and all life is blotted out—except for the seed of a new creation, floating in the ark with Noah and his family.

Noah: One Righteous Man

What do we know about Noah? The Scriptures tell us that he is a tenth-generation descendant of Adam in the line of Seth. In contrast to the great wickedness that was all around him (Gn 6:5), Noah dares to live a different kind of life. He is "a righteous man" who was "blameless in his generation." He was a man who "walked with God" in the midst of a corrupt culture (Gn 6:9). Thus, Noah "found favor in God's eyes" (Gn 6:8)—an expression used to describe someone to whom much will be entrusted (see Gn 39:4). This certainly applies to Noah: Indeed, he is about to be entrusted with the future of the whole human family!

In many ways, the flood narrative presents a kind of re-creation, with language that reflects images from the creation story in Genesis 1 and 2. We see this, for example, with the recurrence of the number seven. Just as God created the world and rested on the seventh day (Gn 2:3), so the new creation with Noah and the flood highlights the number seven several times. The story mentions *seven* pairs of clean animals in the ark (Gn 7:2); *seven* pairs of birds in the ark (Gn 7:3); *seven* days before God sends the rain upon the earth (Gn 7:4); *seven* days before Noah sends out the dove (Gn 8:10); and then *seven* more days before he sends out the dove again (Gn 8:12). Finally, the text points out how the ark came to rest on Mount Ararat in the *seventh* month—reminiscent of how God rested on the seventh day of creation (Gn 8:4).

All these occurrences of the number seven in this short account highlight how the flood is not only bringing punishment upon the earth but also bringing about new life, a new hope, and a new creation through a new covenant.

So if there's a renewed creation with the flood, what would Noah's role be in this new world? Noah is like a new Adam, the new head of the human family. Once again, notice the parallels in the Biblical text: Just as Adam is blessed by God, so Noah is blessed by God. Just as Adam was called to "be fruitful and multiply, and fill the earth" (Gn 1:28), so Noah is called to "be fruitful and multiply, and fill the earth" (Gn 9:1). And both Adam and Noah were tillers of the soil and given dominion over all the animals (Gn 1:28; 2:15; 9:2, 20).

It is inspiring to see what God can do with one righteous man who dares to go against the grain of a corrupt society and live truly for Him. Noah "found favor" in God's eyes, and God used him to renew all of creation. Imagine what God could do with just a few righteous men and women today to help bring new life to a parish, to a campus, or to an organization. Will the way that you live your life find favor in God's eyes? Will you have the kind of impact on the world that God's righteous people in Genesis did?

Chapter Three
More Troubled Waters
Noah's Family Breakdown after the Flood
(Genesis 9-11)

Our next stop on our journey through the Bible reminds us that even righteous men like Noah always need to be on guard, careful not to fall into sin. Though Noah was a heroic man, he too stumbled, and his sin had dramatic consequences for the entire human family.

In the last chapter, we saw how Noah is established as the new Adam—a tiller of the soil, a covenant mediator of God's blessing, commissioned to be fruitful and multiply, and the father of the renewed human family after the flood. But not all the parallels with Adam are desirable. Just as the beginning of humanity was marred by Adam's sin in the Garden of Eden, so the beginning of this new human family is tainted by Noah's sin in the vineyard.

And note the similarities: As a tiller of the soil, Adam sinned in a garden by taking the fruit of the tree, and his shame was exposed in nakedness. Similarly, Genesis 9 shows that Noah was a tiller of the soil who sinned in the vineyard by taking too much fruit of the vine, and his shame is also exposed in nakedness (Gn 9:20-23).

The account of Noah's fall in Genesis 9 is shocking not only because of its disheartening report of Noah's sin, but also because of the surprising punishment given to Noah's grandson, Canaan. Consider the account:

> Noah was the first tiller of the soil. He planted a vineyard; and he drank of the wine, and became drunk, and lay uncovered in his tent. And Ham, the father of Canaan, saw the nakedness of his father, and told his two brothers outside. Then Shem and Japheth took a garment, laid it upon both their shoulders, and walked backward and covered the nakedness of their father; their faces were turned away, and they did not see their father's nakedness. When Noah awoke from his wine and knew what his youngest son had done to him, he said "Cursed be Canaan…." (Gn 9:20-24)

What just happened here? Noah got drunk and his son Ham looked upon his nakedness, so when Noah woke up he cursed Canaan, *his own grandson*! What is the meaning of this strange story?

Cursing Canaan?

In order to understand Noah's anger, we first need to consider what it means that Ham "looked upon the nakedness of his father." When the Bible deals with delicate sexual matters, it frequently uses guarded language. For example, when the Scriptures mean to tell us that Adam and Eve had marital relations, it reads, "Adam knew Eve his wife" (Gn 4:1). The meaning of this idiom is obvious for the mature reader but remains veiled to the young and innocent.

Meanwhile, the scene depicted in Genesis 9 employs similarly veiled language, but to talk about something unnatural and heinous. When Genesis 9:22 says that Ham "saw the nakedness of his father," this is no mere indiscretion, like seeing his father bathing. That wouldn't merit Ham's being cursed, much less Ham's son Canaan.

As the context of this passage doesn't reveal much about its possible meaning, we turn to another approach for interpreting difficult texts: looking at the broader Biblical context. In order to understand the meaning of this expression, we should investigate how "looking upon the nakedness" of one's father is used elsewhere in the Bible. And when we do so, we discover that the idiom denotes something quite appalling. In Leviticus 20:11, this expression is used to describe the condemned act of maternal incest: "The man who lies with his father's wife has uncovered his father's nakedness."[7]

Sexual Sin and Political Power

But why would Ham want to commit incest with his mother? And why would he choose this particular moment of his father's vulnerability, when Noah was intoxicated? This might have been a sin of passion, but it was almost certainly an act of rebellion against the authority of his father and his oldest brother, Shem.

Let's consider the historical context. We've already seen how, after the flood, God gave Noah the mission of ruling over the entire world. In the time of the patriarchs in the Book of Genesis, this authority would be passed on to his eldest son, Shem. Ham is Noah's youngest son and would not be the successor—unless he were to usurp that power through deceit and violence.

As strange as it may seem to the modern reader, this idea of seizing authority by having sexual relations with the ruler's wife is not unprecedented in the ancient word. When foreign invaders toppled other kingdoms, they typically took the previous king's wives for their own, showing that they had authority over everything the king had once possessed. We see this also in the history of Israel, when King David's son Absalom tries to usurp the throne from his father. After Absalom takes over the capital city of Jerusalem, one of his first acts is to take David's concubines and have sexual relations with them in public (see 2 Sm 16:21-22).

The explanation of incest also makes sense of Noah's response. Ham's son Canaan is cursed by Noah—not for anything he had done, but for his father's action. The context would indicate that Canaan—who was the fruit of this incestuous, rebellious union—would suffer the effects of his father's sin, just as Cain's children bore the effects of the curse laid on Cain when he rejected God.[8]

Noah's sin has consequences. His drunkenness opened the door for Ham to make his move, and as a result, Noah's family is left in shambles. Noah's descendants were destined to represent a renewed human family, united in the blessing of God's covenant. But the narrative of Noah and the flood ends in tragedy, with his own son Ham rebelling and Ham's descendants being cursed.

The account of Noah's sin is surprising in another way. After the flood, the human family is given a new land, a renewed creation, a fresh start. We might expect that, with all these changes, men and women would flourish. But the Biblical narrative reveals that the problems facing humanity run much deeper. Noah and his children still struggle with sin and suffer the division and unhappiness that flow from not living in accord with God's plan.

We, too, might sometimes think that all we need is a fresh start—a new city, a new job, some new clothes, maybe some new friends—to get our lives on track and find happiness. But the Scriptures teach that no mere cosmetic change will satisfy our deepest desires. Our problems are not just outside us, they are most fundamentally rooted within us: our weaknesses, fears, insecurities, and sins. Like Noah and his children, we need more than a new environment or a new situation; we need God and His healing power to transform us, so that we can begin to walk in His ways. Only then will we experience the joy and fulfillment in life for which God made us.

CHAPTER FOUR
THREE PROMISES THAT CHANGED THE WORLD
Abraham and God's Covenant Family Plan
(Genesis 10-12)

The Bible next introduces a man who will eventually become one of the most important figures in salvation history: Abram, who will come to be known as Abraham. So critical is Abraham's role in salvation history that the New Testament calls him "the father of all who believe" (Rom 4:11). As we watch God lead this good man to total trust and heroic faithfulness, we will learn what it really means to walk with God and entrust our entire lives to His plan.

In setting up the story of Abraham, Genesis 10 gives us the most extensive genealogy in the Bible so far: a long list of seventy names. Commonly known as the "Table of Nations," this genealogy traces the descendants of Noah through his three sons: Japheth, Ham, and Shem. It serves as one of the most foundational passages in the Bible for understanding the rest of salvation history. Many of the nations that will come from these seventy descendants will play an important role in the drama that unfolds in the rest of Scripture.

All in the Family

Let's take a closer look at two important themes found in this genealogy. Ancient Israelites would have been horrified by many of the names and locations in the segment of Noah's genealogy that lists the descendants of his rebellious son Ham (Gn 10:6-20). While Abram and the nation of Israel were descendants of Noah's faithful first-born son, Shem, the names listed as the descendants of Ham represented some of Israel's most hated enemies.

Imagine how an ancient Israelite would have felt reading Genesis 10:6, which describes Ham as having two sons named Egypt and Canaan. The first son is the patriarch of a nation that would one day enslave Israel for 400 years; the latter fathers a nation that would come to oppose Israel with all its might when the Israelites return to the Promised Land.

Moreover, Genesis 10:10-11 associates Babel and Assyria with the line of Ham. Assyria vanquished ten of the twelve tribes of Israel and sent them into exile in 722 B.C., while Babel later became the home of the Babylonians, who destroyed Jerusalem and carried off the remaining two tribes into slavery in 586 B.C. The genealogy goes on to list other Israelite enemies that flow from Ham's line, including the Philistines (Gn 10:14), the Jebusites and Amorites (Gn 10:16), and Sodom and Gomorrah (Gn 10:19).

This would have been a difficult genealogy for the ancient Israelites to read, with so many of their enemies gathered into this one, long family tree.

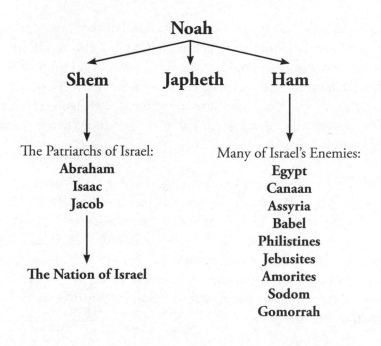

The genealogy, however, serves a second purpose, as it points to an even deeper truth. Long before these warring nations were *enemies*, they were actually *relatives*. So the genealogy would challenge readers to see that these foreign adversaries were not just foes of Israel, but also brothers and sisters—distant cousins in the broken family of Noah. Genesis 10 thus might be seen as challenging the Israelites to view these nations not with vengeance, but ultimately with love and mercy and a desire for healing and restoration in the divided family of man.

Tower of Babel

The Table of Nations in Genesis 10 immediately precedes the account of the Tower of Babel in Genesis 11. This tragic story serves as a prime example of the rebellion and division of the human family. Here we see an early city being built "in the land of Shinar" (Gn 11:2)—an ominous note, since this region was last mentioned as being occupied by the rebellious descendants of Ham (Gn 10:10).

Now, worse things are about to happen here. In Genesis 11:4, the people of Babel say, "Come, let us build ourselves a city, and a tower with its top in the heavens, and let us make a name for ourselves, lest we be scattered abroad upon the face of the whole earth." Their desire to build a city in order to make a name for themselves is reminiscent of the way Cain's descendants built a city in order to glorify their own name, as we saw earlier in Genesis 4:17.

The passage takes on an even more ominous meaning when we understand that the Hebrew word for "name" is *shem*—the name of Noah's first-born son and heir. As the eldest son of Noah, Shem would have been given the role as head patriarch of the covenantal family when his father died. But now, the descendants of Ham in Babel seek to make a name, a "shem," for themselves. This does not mean that they are striving for fame; rather, they are rejecting the blessed line of Shem and wanting to set up a ruler for themselves. We have already seen in the previous chapter that Ham himself tried to overthrow Shem when he "looked upon his father's nakedness." Now,

Ham's descendants continue their father's rebellion as they reject God and the blessed line of Shem, striving to make a name, a "shem," for themselves.

What's more, the people in Babel put themselves in the place of God, using God-like language reminiscent of Genesis 1:26 where God said, "Let us make man in our image after our own likeness." Three times the people in Babel say, "*Let us* make bricks.... *Let us* build a city.... *Let us*...make a name for ourselves" (Gn 11:3-4, emphasis added). They desire to build a rebellious, secular civilization united around their own name and the tower they are building; they are truly building "the city of man." But God comes back with a final "let us" as He muddles their language and scatters the people: "Come, *let us* go down and confuse their language, that they may not understand each other's speech" (Gn 11:7).

Three Promises that Changed the World

Genesis 10 and 11 clearly underscore the division of the human family that results from breaking covenant with God. But during the rebellion of Ham's descendants, at least some in the godly line of Shem continue to follow the Lord all the way down to the tenth generation, in which we meet a man named Abram, who is dwelling in "Ur of the Chaldeans." Here, salvation history takes a dramatic step forward, as God calls this man to follow Him in faith. "Now the Lord said to Abram, 'Go from your country and your kindred and your father's house to the land that I will show you'" (Gn 12:1).

God desires to reunite all the nations into one covenant family through Abram and his descendants, which He will accomplish in three stages, summed up in the three promises. These three promises provide an outline for the rest of salvation history, a table of contents for the rest of the Bible:

> And I will make of you a great nation, and I will bless you, and make your name great, so that you will be a blessing. I will bless those who bless you, and him who curses you I will curse; and by you all the families of the earth shall bless themselves. (Gn 12:2-3)

These three promises not only have great meaning for Abram; they prophetically point toward the most significant turning points in all of human history:

1. First, God promises that Abram will become a great *nation*.
2. Second, God says he will make Abram's *name* great.
3. And finally, God foretells how the *entire* human family will be blessed through Abram.

Let's take a closer look at these three promises, and we will see how Genesis 12 is God's answer to the problem of humanity's division in Genesis 10 and 11.

The Three Promises to Abram

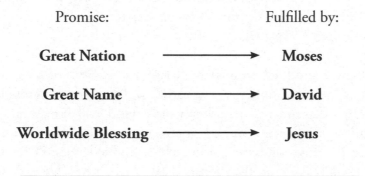

Promise:		Fulfilled by:
Great Nation	⟶	**Moses**
Great Name	⟶	**David**
Worldwide Blessing	⟶	**Jesus**

The promise that Abram will become a *great nation* points to the Exodus story, where his descendants, the Israelites, will be delivered out of slavery in Egypt. At the beginning of the book of Exodus, Israel had become a great and numerous people, but without a land of their own. It is only when Moses leads the Israelites to freedom and to the Promised Land that they can finally rule themselves and become a great nation, thus fulfilling this first promise made to Abram.

The second promise about God giving Abram a *great name* will be fulfilled in King David's dynasty, when the universal importance of the kingdom of Israel will be established for the ages. In the Scriptures, this "great name" is royal language referring both to personal fame and to possessing a name that endures through the centuries, because it is associated with a lasting dynasty (see Ps 72:17). To reign as king in Jerusalem, one had to be a descendant of David and possess David's royal family *name*. This point is reinforced when God first established

David as king and said to him, "I will make for you a great name" (2 Sm 7:9)—thus showing how David's dynasty is the fulfillment of God's promise to Abram to make his family's "name great" (Gn 12:2).

The third and final promise is that of a *worldwide blessing*, in which "all the families of the earth" will be blessed through Abram's descendants. In other words, God will use Abram's family as His instrument for bringing blessing to all the nations on earth. This promise will ultimately be fulfilled in Jesus Christ, who, while living in the Promised Land as a royal descendant of David, will become the savior of the world, reuniting the scattered and divided families of the earth back into the one universal covenant family of God.

A great nation. A royal dynasty. And becoming the instrument for bringing God's blessing to the whole world. That's a lot to be promised in one short conversation with the Lord!

But Abram must go on a long journey if his family is to receive these great blessings—and the journey is not merely a physical one. True, Abram will need to leave his home in Mesopotamia and travel to an unfamiliar land in Canaan. But the more challenging journey for Abram will take place deep inside him—a *spiritual* journey of walking ever more closely with the Lord. As we will see in the next chapter, Abram is led step by step to entrust more of his life to God and to surrender to the mystery of God's plan for him.

CHAPTER FIVE
WALK BY FAITH, NOT BY SIGHT
The Call of Abraham
(Genesis 12-15)

Put yourself in Abram's sandals: He is asked by God to leave his land and his extended family to go to a far away, unfamiliar place. What's more, this new country would not be expected to be a warm and welcoming one for Abram, since it is a land inhabited by the Canaanites—descendants of Ham and rivals to Abram's great ancestor Shem (Gn 12:5, 10:6).

Nevertheless, Abram takes this big leap of faith, trusting in God's plan for him. At the age of 75, he uproots his family, travels to this new land, and worships God there, building altars for the Lord and calling on God's name (Gn 12:4-9).

But this is just the first step of Abram's walk with the Lord. All throughout his life, Abram will be invited by God to take increasingly larger leaps of faith. Through various trials and ordeals, Abram will learn to surrender more of his life to the Lord and to trust ever more in God's care for his life.

We see those tests beginning as soon as he arrives in Canaan. Let's consider four trials that Abram faced in his early days in the land and observe how these ordeals challenge him to trust in the Lord like never before.

Trial No. 1: Famine

After arriving in this land, Abram faces his first unexpected ordeal. A great famine breaks out, and he has to put his family through another major relocation, this time to Egypt—where another rival descendant of Ham dwells (see Gn 12:10, 10:6).

Imagine the soul-searching Abram must have done. Back in the land of Ur, he convinced his family that God called him to move to a foreign country where he will be blessed. And yet, upon their arrival, they experience famine, not blessing. His family may have been tempted to question the authenticity of Abram's calling, or to question the goodness or the power of God. Abram himself may have begun to wonder why things didn't turn out the way he had expected.

Trial No. 2: Pharaoh

But the famine is only the beginning of Abram's troubles. He faces a second and more personal trial after he arrives in Egypt, when Pharaoh finds Abram's wife, Sarai, attractive and desires her for himself. This not only poses a problem for Abram's marriage but puts his own life at risk: He is worried that Pharaoh will have Abram killed and take Sarai for himself (Gn 12:12).

In fear for his life, Abram does not disclose the truth to Pharaoh about his marriage; instead, he tells Pharaoh that Sarai is his sister (a partial truth, since Sarai is Abram's half-sister; see Gn 20:12). As a result, Pharaoh looks favorably upon Abram and showers him with many gifts, including sheep, oxen, asses, donkeys, and male and female servants (Gn 12:16)—all for the sake of Sarai. These worldly gifts appear to be a great boon for Abram at first—but as we will see later in the narrative, they prove to be a snare, for among these gifts given to Abram is a woman named Hagar, an Egyptian servant with whom Abram will commit adultery (Gn 16).

Trial No. 3: A Lot of Trouble

Abram's third trial comes from within his own family. When Sarai, Abram, and Abram's nephew Lot return to the Promised Land, they bring with them all the wealth they have accumulated, in the form of cattle, silver, and gold. But this prosperity becomes a source of division in the family, as the land is insufficient to sustain both Abram's and Lot's herds together, and so they choose to separate peaceably. Abram again emerges as a man of faith who trusts God to care for him and provide for him: Though Abram is the elder, he generously offers Lot the first choice as they divide the land. "And Lot lifted up his eyes, and saw that the Jordan valley was well watered everywhere like the garden of the Lord…. So Lot chose for himself all the Jordan valley" (Gn 13:10-11).

In the ancient near East, it would have been shocking to see Lot, the younger kinsman, take advantage of his elder's gracious offer and keep the best portion of the land for himself, leaving his uncle Abram with the leftovers. And while Lot seems to have chosen the "better" part of the land at first—a beautiful, well-watered valley appearing as spectacular as the garden of Eden—the narrative goes on to highlight how Lot actually makes a very poor decision.

Our first indication that Lot is in trouble comes when, after having chosen this land, we are told that Lot "journeyed east" (Gn 13:11)—reminiscent of Adam and Eve (who were exiled to the east of the garden) as well as Cain, the last person explicitly portrayed as journeying east (Gn 4:16). We also discover that the land Lot chose is populated by the people of "Sodom and Gomorrah" (Gn 13:10), whom the Table of Nations already presented as descendants of the unfaithful line of Ham (Gn 10:19), and whom Genesis 19 shows will be destroyed for their grave immorality. Notice how the narrative casts a shadow over Lot's decision to put himself in a compromising position for the sake of the material benefits of this land: "Lot dwelt among the cities of the valley and moved his tent as far as Sodom. *Now the men of Sodom were wicked, great sinners against the Lord*" (Gn 13:13, emphasis added).

Trial No. 4: 'World War I'

When war later breaks out in the Jordan valley, four kings and their armies overtake five kings and *their* armies and capture Lot in the process (Gn 14:1-12). Though Abram is a man of peace, he is called to take up arms to rescue his nephew. That Abram does this is impressive, especially because Lot had just taken advantage of him by hoarding the best part of the land.

Feel the weight of all that has happened to Abram since he first trusted God and left his home: a famine breaks out; he is forced to relocate to Egypt; the mighty Pharaoh makes advances on his wife; he returns to the land of Canaan, where his nephew Lot takes the better part of the land; Lot is captured in a great battle, and Abram has to rescue him. His obedience to God seems to have landed him in one trial after another. Abram may be considered a living example of what the great sixteenth-century mystic St. Teresa of Avila meant when she said, "Lord, if this is how you treat your friends, it is no wonder you have so few of them!"

Count the Stars

In Genesis 15, Abram finally expresses his frustration for the first time. The Lord appears to him and offers a reward: "Fear not, Abram, I am your shield; your reward shall be very great" (Gn 15:1). An offer that would make any one of us thrilled actually leaves Abram confounded. He is rich with wealth, livestock, and possessions, and yet his material prosperity only underscores the one problem that has haunted him for years: He is advanced in age and continues to be childless. God's offer to reward Abram only highlights more acutely how he has no one in the next generation with whom to share these blessings. Abram sadly responds, "O Lord God, what will thou give me, for I continue childless" (Gn 15:2). He must have had in mind the first promise God made to him many years ago: that his descendants would become a great nation (Gn 12:2). At this stage in his life, however, Abram must have wondered whether that promise would ever be fulfilled. How would his family become a great nation if he didn't have a single descendant to become his heir?

Walk by Faith, Not by Sight

God next does something that will challenge Abram to view the difficulties in his life from a more spiritual perspective, and to trust that God is faithful and truly with him in the midst of his trials. Most of all, Abram needs to trust that God will be faithful to His promise, even if he cannot see from his human perspective how it will all work out. It took great faith for Abram to leave his homeland for the land of Canaan, but God wants to form Abram into a man of even greater faith.

God calls Abram out of his tent and says, "Look toward heaven, and number the stars, if you are able to number them…. So shall your descendants be" (Gn 15:5). This moment has a profound impact on Abram's faith. The Bible says that Abram "believed the Lord; and he reckoned it to him as righteousness" (Gn 15:6).

Why this sudden transformation in faith? Why did Abram's attitude abruptly change from doubt and discouragement to strong belief in God's promise that he will have a son? The Bible gives one small detail in this account that sheds light on the nature of Abram's newfound faith. The narrative tells us that, sometime after Abram counted the stars in the sky, "the sun was going down" (Gn 15:12). Remember that God told Abram to "number the stars, if you are able to number them" (Gn 15:5)—but notice, God asked him to do this before the sun was set. In other words, God asked Abram to count the stars *in broad daylight.*

This radically changes our perception of this scene. At first glance, many readers might envision Abram walking out into a clear desert night with millions of stars in the sky and that, while viewing these countless stars, he comes to believe that God will number his descendants in a similar way. But this one small detail about the sunset coming *after* Abram was told to count the stars means that Abram actually walked outside in the middle of the day, when he could not see anything but the sun!

From this perspective, Abram's extraordinary faith becomes much more apparent. God was asking Abram to have faith in what he could not see. Abram knows the stars are there in the sky, even though he cannot see them, and now he realizes that God is calling him to have similar faith in His promise that he would have many descendants—even though he cannot yet see a single son. As St. Paul says, "Faith is the assurance of things hoped for, the conviction of things not seen" (Heb 11:1).

This is a pivotal moment in Abram's walk with the Lord, but God has a lot more work to do with him. As we will see in the next chapter, Abram will be challenged to entrust his entire life to the Lord—holding nothing back, not even the beloved son whom God would give him. And through this final call to total self-giving, Abram will be molded into the man who will become the premier model of faith in the entire Old Testament.

CHAPTER SIX
SACRIFICING THE BELOVED SON?
Abraham, the Father of Faith
(Genesis 16-22)

We have seen Abram's great faith; now we must look at his great sin, as well as its long-term effects. For many modern readers of the Old Testament, the patriarchs and other heroes in the Bible appear to break the moral code without any reprimand from God. That seems to be the case with Abram in Genesis 16: Abram has intimate relations with a woman named Hagar, who is not his wife, and yet he seemingly goes unpunished.

While Abram came to believe that God would give him a child (Gn 15:6), he still doubts that this promised child will come through his own marriage. After many years of marriage and no children, Abram's wife, Sarai, appears to be too old to conceive. Even she admits this and says to Abram, "Behold now, the Lord has prevented me from bearing children; go into my maid; it may be that I shall obtain children by her" (Gn 16:2). Abram heeds Sarai's advice and has relations with Hagar, her Egyptian maid, and Hagar conceives a son named Ishmael.

This is a clear act of adultery, and yet Abram's sin seems to be unnoticed by God. However, a closer reading of the biblical narrative reveals God's fatherly discipline. The son conceived from this extramarital affair becomes a point of contention in Abram's family, causing discord between Hagar and Sarai (Gn 16 and 21). The rest of Biblical history shows how this marital infidelity sows seeds of division throughout the generations, all the way up to the present day. Ishmael, the son of Hagar through Abram's act of adultery, is considered a founding father of the Arabs; while Isaac, the son of God's promise eventually born to Sarai, will become the father of the Israelites.

For thousands of years, these descendants of Isaac and Ishmael—the Jews and Arabs—have been in perpetual conflict. For the ancient Israelites, this account of Abram and Hagar would have been a painful reminder of the tragic consequences of Abram's marital infidelity.

Getting Away with Adultery?

Moreover, the biblical narrative highlights God's displeasure with Abram's adultery. Up until this time, God has been actively involved in Abram's life (Gn 12-15), but after Abram's liaison with Hagar, the Bible records no discourse between God and Abram for thirteen long years. Then, when God finally speaks to Abram, the Lord's first words challenge him to live by a high moral standard: "I am God Almighty; walk before me, and be blameless" (Gn 17:1). Abram's virtue must be on par with his heroic ancestors Enoch and Noah, who "walked with God" and were "blameless" (Gn 5:22, 6:9).

Abram is ninety-nine years old when God appears to him in this scene (Gn 17:1). In awe and reverence before the presence of the Almighty God, Abram "fell on his face" in worship, humbly lying prostrate (Gn 17:3). God assures Abram that His covenant is still with him and that he will really become the father of a multitude of nations. To underscore this promise, God changes his name—up until this point, he had been known as Abram—to Abraham, which literally means "the father of a multitude" (Gn 17:4-5). The Lord goes on to tell Abraham that he will be the father of great kings who will play an important role in God's covenant plan: "I will make nations of you, and kings shall come forth from you. And I will establish my covenant between me and you and your descendants after you throughout their generations for an everlasting covenant" (Gn 17:6-7).

At this moment, Abraham must be thinking that his many descendants will come through Ishmael, but much to Abraham's surprise, God says these promises of kings and nations will be bestowed on a child given to Sarai. First, God changes Sarai's name to Sarah, which means "princess," highlighting her association with the future kingdom promised to Abraham's heirs. God then emphasizes how the covenantal promise will be carried out not through his adulterous relationship with Hagar, but through Sarah, Abraham's wife.

> I will bless her, and moreover I will give you a son by her; I will bless her, and she shall be a mother of nations; kings of peoples shall come from her. (Gn 17:16)

This pronouncement is abruptly interrupted by Abraham, who once again "fell on his face" (Gn 17:17), but this time he is not doing so out of worship: He is falling on his face in laughter! If Abraham doubted his wife could conceive a child thirteen years earlier, when he committed adultery with Hagar, the prospect of a ninety-year-old Sarah bearing a child now seems ridiculous to him. He says to himself, "Shall a child be born to a man who is a hundred years old? Shall Sarah, who is ninety years old, bear a child?" (Gn 17:17). He then proposes to God that Ishmael be his heir: "Oh, that Ishmael might live in thy sight!" (Gn 17:18).

But God is not laughing. The Lord reminds Abraham that He always intended the promised child to come from his marriage, not from adultery: "No, but Sarah your wife shall bear you a son, and you shall call his name Isaac. I will establish my covenant with him" (Gn 17:19). God will bless Ishmael, too, but the covenant and the promise of future kings will remain with Isaac (Gn 17:20-21).

There is great irony in the name God instructs Abraham to give to this child: Isaac in Hebrew literally means "he laughs." Every time Abraham calls his son, he will be reminded of how he laughed incredulously when God said Sarah would conceive. Though Abraham initially laughed at God's promise, in the end, God will get the last laugh.

Circumcision

In this scene, God also gives Abraham a new covenantal sign: circumcision. God instructs Abraham, "You shall be circumcised in the flesh of your foreskins, and it shall be a sign of the covenant between me and you" (Gn 17:11).

Many modern readers think of circumcision in the Bible as simply an ancient religious ritual, but it was more than that. It was a sign of the "everlasting covenant" God made with Abraham that day (Gn 17:13). As Israel's history unfolds, it will serve as an important sign marking out the descendants of Abraham who are in covenant with God.

This particular sign probably also served as a painful reminder of Abraham's lack of trust in God's promise and his sin with Hagar that followed. In Genesis 16, Abraham committed adultery with Hagar; in the very next chapter, he is commanded by God to be blameless and to be circumcised. Think about what this would mean for Abraham: Here he is, a ninety-nine-year-old man, being told to cut off the flesh of his foreskin. Abraham might have been wondering, "Why can't I receive a rainbow for a sign, Lord…like Noah?" For Abraham, circumcision probably would have felt, at least on some level, like a punishment—and the punishment fits the crime.

This ritual might also be seen as another test of Abraham's faith: On the heels of the fresh wound of circumcision, this elderly man and his barren wife are to have a son within a year? From a natural perspective, Abraham and Sarah have never before been *less* capable of fulfilling their call to become parents. The story reminds us that, with God, nothing is impossible. Abraham is being called to trust in God's ability to overcome any obstacle.

The Final Test

Even after God finally gives Sarah a child named Isaac (Gn 21:1-3), Abraham must face the climactic test of his faith. God says to Abraham, "Take your son, your only son Isaac, whom you love, and go to the land of Moriah, and offer him there as a burnt offering upon one of the mountains of which I shall tell you" (Gn 22:2).

This request is almost incomprehensible. Imagine a man now in his second century who has waited his entire life for his wife to bear him a son. He probably loved nothing on this earth more than Isaac—and yet the Lord comes to Abraham and tells him he must be willing to give up even this, his very own son.

Nevertheless, Abraham obeys the Lord. He rises the next morning, cuts wood for the sacrifice, saddles his donkey, and travels with his son to Moriah just as God commanded. Once they get there, they ascend the mountain, with Isaac carrying the wood for the sacrifice on his shoulders. At the top of the mountain, Abraham prepares the altar, binds Isaac. and lays his son on the altar of wood. This most weighty sacrifice is ready to begin.

Just at that moment, an angel from heaven intervenes, saying, "Abraham, Abraham!... Do not lay your hand on the lad or do anything to him; for now I know that you fear God, seeing you have not withheld your son, your only son, from me" (Gn 22:11-12).

Here we finally see Abraham's faith perfected. Throughout his life, Abraham has been willing to follow God, but not totally. Afraid of putting his life completely in God's hands, Abraham doubted God's promises (Gn 15:2-3) and pursued his own plans rather than God's ways (16:2-4). But here, finally, Abraham puts everything on the altar, holding nothing back—not even his beloved son—from God. He trusts in the Lord, who promised him, "Through Isaac shall your descendants be named" (Gn 21:12), even though he has no idea *how* God will keep His promise if Isaac is sacrificed. Abraham has come to trust that God *will* do so somehow, even if that meant He would have to raise Isaac from the dead (see Heb 11:17-19).

The account ends with God making an amazing covenant oath to Abraham, swearing to bless all the nations through his family: "And by your descendants shall all the nations of the earth bless themselves" (Gn 22:18). Abraham's family will become the instrument God uses to reunite in God's blessing the entire divided and rebellious human family. In fact, this covenant oath relates to the third of the three promises God made to Abraham all the way back in Genesis 12:3: the promise for the worldwide blessing ("and by you all the families of the earth shall bless themselves").

The Faith of Isaac

Many commentators on this passage focus on the faith of Abraham, but not as many consider the tremendous faith Isaac must have had. Imagine what Isaac was going through when he saw his own father tie him up, lay him on the altar, and pull out a knife to slay him!

One interesting aspect of this account is that Isaac may have been in his teens at this time. He certainly was old enough to carry the wood up the mountain and to understand the intricacies for the kind of sacrifice being offered (Gn 22:7). If he could do that, he probably was wise and strong enough to run away when he saw what was happening or resist his elderly father, who was over one hundred years at the time. This perspective would shed light on what a number of ancient Jewish rabbis and early Christians just assumed: that Isaac was a voluntary victim who willingly submitted to be sacrificed. In this view, Isaac freely chose to obey God's command, even if that meant his own death. What amazing faith Isaac must have had!

But as heroic as Abraham and Isaac's faith might have been, this passage is more than a story of heroic obedience: It also foreshadows how God will bring his saving plan for all humanity to completion. The particulars of this story prefigure what will happen in this same place some two thousand years later, when Jesus Christ dies on the cross. Consider how the following details from this scene relate to Christ's own sacrifice on Calvary: the mountain, the beloved son, the donkey, the sacrificial wood, and the voluntary sacrifice.

The location of Abraham's sacrifice—Mount Moriah—is significant because it was a sacred place that later came to be associated with Jerusalem (see 2 Chron 3:1 and Ps 76:1-3).

Just as Abraham went to offer his only beloved son, Isaac, on Mount Moriah, so did God the Father offer his only beloved Son on Calvary, which came to be known as one of the hills of Moriah.

Similarly, just as Isaac traveled up to Moriah on a donkey, so did Jesus ride a donkey up to Jerusalem a few days before He died. Like Isaac, who shouldered the wood for the sacrifice up the mountain, Jesus also carried the sacrificial wood—the wood of the cross—up to Calvary on Good Friday. Finally, Jesus willingly stretched out His hands, laid His body on the wood, and allowed Himself to be bound to the cross and offered in sacrifice—harkening back to Isaac's offering of himself on that same mountain.

Here we see how, in the Bible, God uses more than words to communicate His plan of salvation. God doesn't just tell Abraham that the whole world will be blessed through him; He *shows* Abraham—and us—how He will do it. In this way, the suspenseful event of Abraham's sacrifice of his only beloved son on Mount Moriah serves as a ritually enacted statement about how God will bring His plan of salvation to completion through the sacrifice of His only beloved Son, Jesus Christ, on the mountain in Jerusalem on Good Friday.

CHAPTER SEVEN
ALWAYS REACHING FOR MORE
How Jacob's Schemes Catch Up to Him
(Genesis 23-36)

The next major figure in our journey through the Bible is Abraham's grandson Jacob (the son of Isaac)—a man who stands in contrast with Abraham himself, the great father of faith. While Abraham comes to place all his trust in God, Jacob is introduced as a schemer who aggressively pursues his own desires for his life, even if they are not in accord with God's plan. He swindles his brother Esau's birthright, steals Esau's blessing, and dishonorably violates custom as he seeks to marry a younger daughter before the firstborn is given in marriage. Jacob relies on his own plotting and effort more than he relies on God. It's no wonder that his name will be changed to "Israel," which means "he who strives with God" (Gn 32:28).

But God will still work with Jacob and write straight with Jacob's crooked lines. Despite his weaknesses, Jacob will be entrusted with the great promises and blessing passed down from Abraham and become a great patriarch at the foundation of Israel's history.

Sibling Rivalry

The story of Abraham's family picks up in Genesis 24 when his son Isaac marries a woman named Rebekah, who conceives twin sons that are rivals from the start as they "struggled together" in her womb (Gn 25:22). Even their birth was a moment of contention: When the firstborn, Esau, was delivered, the second-born grabbed hold of Esau's heel (Gn 25:26)—hence the younger brother was named "Jacob," which means "supplanter" or "cheater," or even more literally, "he clutches the heel." Jacob's heel-grabbing move at birth foreshadows his future strife with Esau: Never content with second place, the heel-grabber at birth will grow up and grab at Esau's privileges as the firstborn son.

First, Jacob grabs at Esau's birthright. When Esau returns from hunting one day, he is famished and pleads with Jacob for some food. Seeing an opportunity to best his older brother, Jacob says he will share some pottage with him in exchange for his birthright. The birthright represents his prerogatives and status as the firstborn son, including the right to a double portion of the inheritance that his father would award each son. In a moment of rash desperation, Esau agrees and exchanges half his inheritance for a pottage of lentils (Gn 25:29-34).

Stolen Blessing

But getting the birthright was not enough for Jacob. He still wants more and grabs at the *blessing* Esau was supposed to receive from his father as well.

What is the difference between the birthright and the blessing? The *birthright* refers to the concrete, material inheritance a firstborn son would receive from the father—the lion's share of the father's estate. The *blessing* is a spiritual inheritance: The father invokes God's grace upon the firstborn so that he can carry out his responsibility to lead his family as patriarch after his father dies. This was an almost king-like function, as his clan would be placed under his care and protection (see Gen 27:29, 37). The firstborn also assumed a priestly role, leading the family in worship and mediating their relationship with God (see Gn 8:20-21, 12:6-8, 15:9-21, 26:23-25).

In Esau's case, he was to receive the most important blessing mentioned in the Book of Genesis, for his father was the guardian of the covenant blessing that came to him from Abraham—a blessing that had its roots in God's blessing of Adam and Eve and was linked with God's promise to give Abraham's descendants a great land (Gn 28:3-4) and to bless the entire human family through them (Gn 28:14). Thus, as Isaac neared his death and prepared to bestow his blessing upon his firstborn son, it would have been the greatest moment in Esau's life:

> When Isaac was old and his eyes were dim so that he could not see, he called Esau his older son, and said to him, "My son"; and he answered, "Here I am." He said, "Behold, I am old; I do not know the day of my death. Now then, take your weapons, your quiver and your bow, and go out to the field and hunt game for me, and prepare for me savory food, such as I love, and bring it to me that I may eat; that I may bless you before I die." (Gn 27:1-4)

It is at this pivotal point in Esau's life that his younger brother Jacob steps in and steals his blessing—the heel-grabbing supplanter living up to his name once again. Jacob quickly puts on Esau's best garments, covering himself with animal skins to make him appear more hairy like his older brother, and brings his father food that Rebekah prepared for him. Jacob thus misleads his father into thinking he is Esau coming for the blessing. The nearly blind Isaac is fooled and gives Jacob the covenantal blessing, elevating him as lord over all of Abraham's family and the spiritual descendants of Abraham's only beloved son:

> Let peoples serve you, and nations bow down to you. Be lord over your brothers, and may your mother's sons bow down to you. Cursed be everyone who curses you, and blessed be everyone who blesses you! (Gn 27:29)

When Esau returns, he is understandably devastated. By rights, *he* should have become the patriarchal father of the blessed line of Abraham and Isaac—but all this has been usurped by his younger brother. Isaac already gave the blessing to Jacob, and there is nothing he can do to take it back. As Isaac explains,

> Behold, I have made him your lord, and all his brothers I have given to him for servants, and with grain and wine I have sustained him. What then can I do for you, my son? (Gn 27:37)

With an enraged Esau now plotting to kill his brother, Rebekah sends Jacob away to her brother Laban in Haran. For Rebekah, this solves two problems in one move: First, she can protect her beloved Jacob from Esau, and second, she can protect Jacob from the pagan immorality in the land. She has already lamented that Esau married two pagan Hittite women, making life bitter for her and Isaac (Gn 26:34-35). She does not want the same to happen to Jacob, so she sends him away, hoping he will find a godly wife among their own Hebrew kinsmen in Haran (Gn 27:42–28:1).

The Younger before the Older

Jacob's sins, however, eventually catch up with him. When Jacob arrives in Haran, he meets Laban's two daughters, Leah and Rachel. Leah, the firstborn, is described as having weak eyes, and her name can be translated "cow." In contrast, Laban's younger daughter, Rachel, is described as "beautiful and lovely," and her name literally means "ewe lamb" (Gn 29:17).

Jacob immediately falls in love with Rachel, but according to custom, the younger sister should not marry before the older one. Nevertheless, Jacob reaches for something that is not supposed to be his: He wants Rachel as his wife, even though her older sister Leah is not yet married. So much did Jacob desire Rachel that he agrees to serve his uncle Laban for seven years in return for Rachel's hand in marriage. "So Jacob served seven years for Rachel, and they seemed to him but a few days because of the love he had for her" (Gn 29:20).

But when the day of the wedding arrives, Laban makes a cunning switch. At the end of the marriage feast that evening, instead of bringing Rachel to Jacob, Laban brings him the elder daughter, Leah. In the dark of night, Jacob consummates his marriage with a woman whom he presumes to be Rachel.

Jacob makes the startling discovery the next day: "And in the morning, behold, it was Leah" (Gn 29:25). That's one big "behold"! In the clearer light of day, Jacob realizes that the daughter he had been given in marriage was not his beloved Rachel but her older, unattractive sister, Leah. The deceiver finds himself deceived; the trickster has been tricked. Jacob has finally gotten a taste of his own medicine.

Outraged, Jacob goes to his father-in-law and objects, "What is this you have done to me? Did I not serve with you for Rachel? Why then have you deceived me?" (Gn 29:25). Ironically, Jacob the arch-deceiver now complains of having been duped himself. In accusing Laban of trickery, Jacob is unwittingly condemning himself.

But Laban's response must have cut Jacob to the heart: "It is not so done in our country, to give the younger before the first-born" (Gn 29:25-6).

Jacob has no response to this. Laban's words probably remind Jacob of his own sin in putting himself before the firstborn Esau back in Canaan. He tried to supplant a firstborn again here in Haran, but Laban says such a horrendous thing "is not so done *in our country.*" The stinging implication is that it should not have been done in Jacob's homeland, either.

Many Wives?

After marrying Leah, Jacob ends up working an additional seven years in exchange for Rachel as his second wife. This is not good news. As we saw in the case of Abraham, a lack of faithfulness to one wife creates tension in the family. In Jacob's case, this rivalry will affect not only his wives but also the sons they bear him.

First, the Lord recognizes that Leah was unloved and blesses her with the ability to conceive children (Gn 29:31). Rachel, who had been incapable of conceiving children of her own, becomes infuriated. She envies her sister Leah so much that she preferred her husband take yet *another* woman rather than concede supremacy to her rival. She offers her maidservant Bilhah to Jacob as a concubine, in the misguided hope that Bilhah somehow will bear children on Rachel's behalf. But when Bilhah conceives, Rachel doesn't defeat her rival; she merely creates a new one. Now there are *two* women who have borne children for her husband.

Not willing to be outdone by Rachel, Leah makes a similar move, offering her maidservant Zilpah as a concubine as well. Zilpah also conceives, only adding to the rivalry. Conflict begins to overwhelm the family.

Finally, God remembers the barren Rachel, and she gives birth to two sons, Joseph and Benjamin. All in all, Jacob fathers twelve sons through four different women. But God's revelation in the Bible shows that polygamy has negative consequences. Though these twelve sons will become known as the twelve patriarchs of the nation of Israel, the Bible also shows that Jacob's sons experience intense rivalry, and tension will arise in the history of their descendants. As we will see in the next chapter, the Bible reveals the long-term heartache that will come as a result of Jacob's departure from God's intention for marriage to be a permanent and exclusive union between one man and one woman.

CHAPTER EIGHT
BRINGING GOOD OUT OF EVIL
The Trials and Exaltation of Joseph
(Genesis 37-50)

The most well-known sibling rivalry in the Book of Genesis comes in the story of Joseph, the firstborn son of Jacob's beloved wife Rachel. Just as Jacob's favoritism toward Rachel caused turmoil in his marriages, his preference for her son, Joseph, causes tension among his many children.

Jacob not only favors Joseph, he dotes on his son in front of Joseph's brothers, inflating their envy to almost murderous levels.

> Now Israel [Jacob] loved Joseph more than any other of his children, because he was the son of his old age; and he made a long robe with sleeves. But when his brothers saw that their father loved him more than all his brothers, they hated him, and could not speak peaceably to him. (Gn 37:3-4)

To make matters worse, Joseph claims to be a visionary who experiences prophetic dreams. When he tells his brothers of dreams he had of them bowing down before him in reverence, the fraternal animosity reaches a fever pitch. This is the straw that breaks the camel's back; the brothers now take Joseph by force and sell him into slavery. To cover up their treacherous deed, they take Joseph's tunic, dip it in blood, and show the blood-stained cloak to their father, tricking Jacob into thinking that his beloved son has been devoured by a wild beast. Notice again how Jacob reaps what he has sown: In his youth, Jacob deceived his own father when he stole the blessing from Esau. Now, in his old age, Jacob is deceived by his *own* children about what has happened to Joseph.

Joseph's Purity

Joseph is a man who, in many ways, is the complete opposite of his father. We saw earlier that Jacob was a schemer who aggressively pursued his own self-interest and grasped at things that were not meant to be his. Instead of trusting in God and His plan for his life, Jacob tended to trust more in his *own* plans, which usually brought more harm than good to him and his family.

Joseph, on the other hand, is a simple, honest man who still rises to great prominence. It's clear that his life is truly guided by the Lord's hand, not his own. Despite suffering many betrayals and persecutions, Joseph remains a man of integrity. God protects him and elevates him to positions far beyond anything his father Jacob could have ever imagined.

After his brothers sell Joseph into slavery, he ends up in the house of a high-ranking Egyptian named Potiphar. There, the Bible tells us, "the Lord was with Joseph," and everything he did prospered (Gen 39:2). Potiphar noticed this and made Joseph the head of his entire household (Gn 39:6).

Things were looking good for Joseph, until Potiphar's wife begins to lust after him. Joseph refuses to give in to her desires, saying, "How then can I do this great wickedness, and sin against God?" (Gn 39:9). Not taking "no" for an answer, Potiphar's wife continues her relentless pursuit, as day after day she asks Joseph to lie with her. Her lust finally turns to aggression when she seizes his garments and pulls him close to herself. Joseph is forced to choose between giving in to her desires or fleeing, leaving only his garment in her grasp. A man of virtue, Joseph chooses to flee, and to this day he is hailed as a model of chastity in the Jewish tradition.

His act of virtue, however, is not appreciated by Potiphar's wife. Humiliated and spurned, she realizes that she will never have her way with him. Her lust turns to anger, and she sets out to destroy Joseph. Using the garment that she stole from him, she accuses Joseph of attempting to rape her. In the face of his wife's accusation, Potiphar throws his faithful servant into prison (Gn 39:7-18).

Falling Upward

Yet the Bible tells us again that "the Lord was with Joseph" even in the midst of this second ordeal (Gn 39:21). Just as Joseph the slave was elevated to head of Potiphar's household, now, as an inmate, he wins the favor of the jailer and becomes the overseer of the entire prison.

> And the keeper of the prison committed to Joseph's
> care all the prisoners who were in the prison…. [T]
> he keeper of the prison paid no heed to anything that
> was in Joseph's care, because the Lord was with him;
> and whatever he did, the Lord made it prosper. (Gn
> 39:22-23)

God's blessing continues to favor Joseph. While in jail, Joseph employs his gift of interpreting dreams for a fellow prisoner who had been the chief butler for Pharaoh's court. When the butler is restored to Pharaoh's good graces and the king starts having strange dreams of his own, the butler informs Pharaoh of Joseph, who is called up from prison to appear before Pharaoh and interpret his dream (Gn 39-41).

Pharaoh's dream foretells dramatic events about to take place in the Middle East. He dreams of seven fat cows coming out of the Nile River, followed by seven gaunt cows that come up and eat the seven fat cows. Joseph explains that the seven fat cows represent seven years of superabundant harvest in the land, while the seven gaunt cows represent seven years of devastating famine that will follow the years of plenty. Joseph goes on to offer Pharaoh wise counsel: Store the grain from the years of plenty, so that Egypt will have enough food during the years of famine.

Just as Potiphar and the chief jailer recognized that the Lord was with Joseph and gave him special authority, Pharaoh too sees the Spirit of God in Joseph (Gn 41:39) and vests him with authority over all of Egypt, making him a prime minister, or "master of the palace," to rule the people on Pharaoh's behalf. Pharaoh says to him, "You shall be over my house, and all my people shall order themselves as you command; only as regards the throne will I be greater than you" (Gn 41:40). To mark his elevation, Pharaoh bestows upon Joseph his signet ring, makes him ride in his second chariot, and instructs all the people to kneel before him. Pharaoh tells him, "I am Pharaoh, and without your consent no man shall lift up hand or foot in all the land of Egypt" (Gn 41:44).

What an amazing day this must have been for Joseph! He wakes up as prisoner in a dungeon and goes to bed that night in a palace, dressed in royal attire and reigning as second in command over all of Egypt. And all this happens without any scheming or vying for power on Joseph's part.

Because of God's blessing, every trouble that befalls Joseph leads to an even *greater* blessing. His brothers sell him into slavery, and he finds himself entrusted with the oversight of Potiphar's house. Potiphar's wife falsely accuses him and he is thrown into prison, but this becomes the opportunity to meet Pharaoh and become Pharaoh's right-hand man—and eventually, as we will now see, the savior of a great multitude.

Family Reunion

Just as Joseph had predicted, the time of abundant harvest ends after seven years, and famine strikes the land. People from all over come to Egypt to buy grain (Gn 41:57), including Joseph's own brothers. Providentially, this leads them right back to the same younger brother whom they betrayed so many years before.

To purchase the grain, the brothers have to go through Joseph, but they do not recognize him. They bow down before him, fulfilling the prophetic dreams of his youth about how he one day would reign over his older brothers and they would bow down before him (Gn 37:5-11, 42:6-9). Joseph, on the other hand, immediately recognizes his brothers but waits to reveal his identity. His love for his family is greater than his anger over having been sent away in slavery, but he uses the occasion to test their character. Joseph accuses the youngest brother, Benjamin, of stealing and threatens to imprison him as a test of the other brothers' loyalty. Years before, they had turned on a younger brother—Joseph himself—but now they demonstrate family allegiance, coming to the defense of Benjamin.

Overwhelmed by their devotion, particularly Judah's willingness to take the place of his younger brother and to be thrown into prison himself, Joseph finally reveals his identity. Reconciled, Joseph and his brothers send for their father and the rest of the family to join them in Egypt (Gn 43-45).

Good from Evil

In Joseph's saga, the Bible highlights how God's providential care is more powerful than our human schemes. And this is a challenge to us: In what will we put our trust? Will we be more like Jacob the schemer and rely on our own plans and efforts? Or will we be more like Joseph, who simply seeks to do what is right and trusts in God to provide for him? We each may have certain plans and dreams for our own life, but Scripture teaches us that God has a plan for us as well. The drama of life is about choosing which plan to trust.

The story of Joseph also addresses one of the most perplexing problems that confronts humanity: the problem of suffering. How can an all-powerful, loving God allow bad things to happen to good people? Though not providing an exhaustive answer to this perennial question, the end of the Book of Genesis sheds some light on how God responds to the suffering of the righteous. The story of Joseph reveals that God is so powerful that He can use the evils of this world to bring about even greater good. As Joseph explains to his own brothers, "You meant evil against me; but God meant it for good, to bring it about that many people should be kept alive" (Gn 50:20). God took the many evils inflicted upon Joseph and used them to bring about a greater good—to bring Joseph to power in Egypt so that he could save his family and many peoples from starvation (see CCC 312). In this sense, Joseph prefigures Jesus Christ: God took the greatest evil in history—the unjust crucifixion of His innocent Son—and used it to bring about the greatest good: the salvation of the human family.

The Blessing of Judah

The Book of Genesis concludes with Jacob gathering his twelve sons around him for a final blessing before he dies. These sons are the patriarchal fathers of the twelve tribes that will make up the nation of Israel. But one particular son, Judah, is given a unique blessing that foretells how God will bring a great king to Israel from Judah's descendants. The promised king in this prophetic blessing is symbolized by a lion and a royal scepter.

Consider Jacob's words to Judah:

> Judah, your brothers shall praise you;
> your hand shall be on the neck of your enemies;
> your father's sons shall bow down before you.
> Judah is a lion's whelp;
> from the prey, my son, you have gone up.
> He stooped down, he couched as a lion,
> and as a lioness; who dares rouse him up?
> The scepter shall not depart from Judah,
> nor the ruler's staff from between his feet,
> until he comes to whom it belongs;
> and to him shall be the obedience of the peoples.
> (Gn 49:8-10)

Here we see the emergence of a royal line from the family of Abraham, Isaac, and Jacob. God's promise to Abraham that kings would arise from his family will be carried out through this particular tribe of Judah. Jacob speaks of Judah's leadership role in the family when he tells how Judah's brothers "shall bow down before you." But Jacob goes on to prophesy something even more amazing: A future royal leader from the tribe of Judah will rule not only over all twelve tribes of Israel, but also over the whole world—"to him shall be the obedience of the peoples" (Gn 49:10).

And who is this king to whom belongs the royal scepter and the obedience of the peoples? Some may see a partial fulfillment of this prophecy in King David, but ultimately, it points to Jesus Christ Himself. He is the lion from the tribe of Judah, as the New Testament reveals (Rv 5:5-6). He is the one to whom belongs the royal scepter and the obedience of all the nations. And so, at the close of the Book of Genesis, we have another foreshadowing of the great king who will establish a worldwide kingdom and gather all humanity back into covenant with God.

CHAPTER NINE
'LET MY PEOPLE GO!'
Israel's Exodus from Egypt
(Exodus 1-23)

Our journey through the big picture of the Bible now takes us to the Book of Exodus—a book that begins with a startling twist. On one hand, the Lord continues to work His covenantal plan for the descendants of Abraham, Isaac, and Jacob, even in the land of Egypt. The first chapter notes that the people were "fruitful" and "multiplied" (Ex 1:7), which recalls what the Bible said about Adam, Noah, and the patriarchs. This underscores how the Israelites continue to share in the same blessing given to their forefathers. Indeed, the small tribe of seventy people that Jacob brought down to Egypt has now, hundreds of years later, "increased greatly" and become "exceedingly strong" (Ex 1:7).

On the other hand, Exodus introduces a new threat to God's covenantal promises when it reports that a new king arises in Egypt "who did not know Joseph" (Ex 1:8).

This lack of "knowing" does not mean that the new Pharaoh was unacquainted with the famous dream interpreter, Joseph, who saved Egypt from famine and became Pharaoh's chief administrator of the kingdom. Rather, in the politics of the day, the expression indicates a fundamental breach in Egypt's relationship with Joseph's family.

The term "to know" (*yadah*) in Hebrew signifies an intimate, covenant friendship with another person (see Gn 29:5, 2 Sm 7:2). The word can describe the profound communion an individual has with God (Ez 24:27, Is 1:3) or the most intimate union between a man and woman (Gn 4:1).

Thus, Exodus 1:8 indicates that, with the rise of this new Pharaoh, Israel's relationship with the Egyptians has been completely ruptured. The new king does not "know" Joseph. This means the descendants of Jacob and Joseph no longer experience close covenant friendship with the Egyptian king. Instead of viewing the Israelites as an ally and a blessing, he views their increasing strength as a threat. He has them enslaved and attempts to destroy them by having every newborn male child thrown into the Nile River (Ex 1:8-21).

God responds to this crisis by sending His people Moses. The circumstances surrounding Moses' birth have great significance, for they foreshadow his future vocation to rescue God's people: Pharaoh's daughter discovers the Hebrew child in a basket floating on the Nile, after his Israelite mother put him there in a desperate attempt to save the child's life. The child's name, Moses, is derived from the Hebrew verb *mashah*, meaning "to draw out of." The one who was saved by being drawn out of the dangerous waters of the Nile will later rescue Israel by drawing the people out of Egypt through the waters of the Red Sea and leading them to the Promised Land.

Ten Strikes against Egypt's Gods

One of the most famous aspects of the Exodus story is the ten plagues that fall on Egypt. Though God (through Moses) commands Pharaoh to let His people go, the Egyptian king repeatedly refuses; as a result, his nation is afflicted by a series of plagues. At first glance, these plagues seem merely intended to make life miserable for the Egyptians and to serve as a punishment for their enslaving the Israelites. However, if we examine these divine acts of judgment in their historical context, we see that they are also intended to help the Egyptians reject their pagan ways and embrace the one, true God.

First, note the theme of "knowing" in the account of Pharaoh and the plagues. When Moses first confronts Pharaoh with God's command to release the people, the king responds, "Who is the Lord, that I should heed his voice and let Israel go? I do not know the Lord, and moreover I will not let Israel go" (Ex 5:2).

Right from the start, Pharaoh obstinately proclaims that he does not "know" the Lord—in other words, he has no intimate relationship with Him—and refuses to let the people go. Yet every time Pharaoh rejects God, his nation is confronted with another plague, whose purpose is to help the stubborn king finally come to know the Lord. In fact, in almost every instance, Moses says each plague is given so that Pharaoh and the Egyptians may "know" the Lord (Ex 7:17; 8:10, 22; 9:29; 10:2). This refrain of *knowing* the Lord tells us that one of the main purposes of the plagues is to lead Egypt to know the one, true God—to recognize the supremacy of Yahweh.

But how do the plagues do this? These plagues are not random acts of retribution; they are strategic. Many scholars have pointed out that the ten plagues are connected with various Egyptian deities. For example, the Nile River, whose waters were a source of life in this region, was associated with various Egyptian gods. The god Osiris ruled the world, and the Nile represented his bloodstream. The Nile-god Hapy was a god of creation and fertility who was linked with the river's annual inundation. There were even songs sung to the Nile, which itself was hailed as a deity: "Hail to thee, O Nile, that issues from the earth and comes to keep Egypt alive!"[9] But in the first plague, when Moses strikes the Nile, it turns to blood, symbolizing judgment on the false gods associated with this river.

Similarly, the Egyptians worshipped the sun god Ra, and in the ninth plague, the sun is darkened for three days, expressing Yahweh's sovereignty over this supreme Egyptian deity. Underlying all of the plagues is a subversion of the Egyptian belief in Pharaoh himself as a god with power over the cosmos. According to Egyptian tradition, Pharaoh was responsible for ensuring that the land was fertile, that the Nile provided water, and that the sun shined its light. With this background, we can see how plagues bringing a darkened sun, destruction of crops, and a bloody, undrinkable, frog-infested Nile River would be a direct attack on Pharaoh's divine attributes. They show that the God of Israel—not Pharaoh—is in control of the cosmos.

More than simply a display of God's wrath, the plagues reveal the dominance of the God of Israel as He exercises divine judgment over the many false gods of the Egyptians (Ex 12:12). This is why God often says that the plagues are given so that "the Egyptians shall know that I am the Lord" (Ex 7:5): Coming to know the Lord would involve recognizing the superiority of Yahweh and rejecting the Egyptian deities, who are powerless in the face of the God of Israel.

Not Forty Years

But the Egyptians are not the only people in the Book of Exodus who need to turn to God. A second key aspect of the Exodus story is the specific plan God has for Israel. It is often thought that God called Moses at the burning bush to lead Israel out of slavery and into the desert on their way to the Promised Land. However, if we take a closer look, we see that God's first concern is to liberate the people from a much deeper form of slavery than their drudgery under Egyptian taskmasters. Listen to what God tells Moses to say to Pharaoh:

> You and the elders of Israel shall go to the king of Egypt and say to him, "The Lord, the God of the Hebrews, has met with us; and now, we pray you, let us go a three days' journey into the wilderness, that we may sacrifice to the Lord our God." (Ex 3:18)

Notice that the message to Pharaoh does not include anything about a permanent liberation, a forty-year journey through the wilderness, or Israel's moving to the Promised Land. This initial request focuses on a short three-day journey, in which the Hebrews will worship God in the desert and then return to Egypt.

Certainly, God's long-term goal is to bring Israel to the land originally promised to Abraham's family (Gn 12:1-3, Ex 3:17). However, the initial need for a three-day journey to sacrifice in the desert may point to a deeper and more profound spiritual crisis in Israel than the problem of slavery under Pharaoh. After the fourth plague, Pharaoh temporarily relents and says he will allow the Hebrews to sacrifice to their God, but they must do so within the land of Egypt. Moses responds by saying that this is not possible:

> It would not be right to do so; for we shall sacrifice to the Lord our God offerings abominable to the Egyptians. If we sacrifice offerings abominable to the Egyptians before their eyes, will they not stone us? We must go three days' journey into the wilderness and sacrifice to the Lord our God as he will command us. (Ex 8:26-27)

Why does Israel need to go out into the wilderness to offer these sacrifices? And why would Moses be so nervous about offering them within the land of Egypt? Moreover, why would Moses say that the Egyptians will *kill* the Israelites if they see the people offering these particular sacrifices?

Moses is probably aware that the animals the Israelites intend to offer in sacrifice were associated with various Egyptian deities. Indeed, according to ancient Jewish interpretations (as well as some of the early Christian writers known as the Church Fathers), God commanded Israel to sacrifice the very animals that represented some of the most prominent gods in the Egyptian cult. For example, the sun goddess, Hathor, was depicted as a cow; the fertility god, Apis, as a bull; the gods Amun and Khnum as rams. Killing these animals that represented Egyptian deities would have been an abomination to the Egyptians. Such an act would have incited a riot and put the lives of the Israelites at risk. For this reason, Israel needed to go a three-day's journey away from the Egyptians to sacrifice these animals in the solitude of the desert.

But why did God want Israel to sacrifice these animals in the first place? On a basic level, such an action expresses a rejection of the Egyptian deities associated with these animals. But there may be something more: The Bible reveals that, after hundreds of years of dwelling in the land of Egypt, the Israelites had not only been living with the Egyptians but also living *like* them, as Egyptian immorality and idolatry had crept into their hearts (see Jos 24:14, Ez 20:7-8). By instructing the people to sacrifice these animals, the Lord was, at least in part, challenging the people to acknowledge Him as the one true God and to renounce any lingering belief in the Egyptian deities represented by these animals. The three-day ceremony would provide the opportunity for the Israelites to repent and realign themselves with the covenant Yahweh established with their forefathers Abraham, Isaac, and Jacob. Here we see that God is not only trying to get Israel out of Egypt, He is also trying to get *Egypt* out of Israel.[10]

The Passover Choice

Even in the face of God's mighty deeds, Pharaoh digs in his heels and refuses to let the people go to the wilderness to worship the Lord. God finally intervenes with one more plague that will be the impetus for the liberation of the people. In this tenth and most devastating plague, all the firstborn sons in Egypt will be killed, except those in households that celebrated a ritual called the Passover. The ritual involved sacrificing an unblemished lamb from their sheep or goats (Ex 12:5) and marking one's doorpost with the blood of the lamb.

Think about how dangerous this would have been for the Israelites: The animals being sacrificed in the Passover—sheep and goats—were associated with Egyptian gods! We just saw how Moses did not want the people to sacrifice such animals in Egypt because he feared it would incite the Egyptians to kill them (Ex 8:25-27). But now, with Pharaoh refusing to let the Israelites take leave, God commands them to sacrifice these animals right in the land of Egypt and then mark their doorposts with the sacrificial blood for all to see. The first Passover, therefore, involves a public renunciation of Egyptian idolatry that challenges the Israelites to make a decisive choice between serving the Lord and serving the Egyptian gods. It marks a key turning point away from their past and starting anew with Yahweh.

Out of Egypt

Imagine the grief and terror of the Egyptians the following morning when they awoke to find all the firstborn sons in Egypt dead, except those sons of the Israelites who had celebrated the Passover the night before. Pharaoh finally relents and lets the people go without any conditions. He drives them from the land, saying, "Go, serve the Lord, as you have said. Take your flocks and your herds, as you have said and be gone" (Ex 12:31-32).

Yet shortly after the Israelites are leaving, Pharaoh has a change of heart. He sends his army after the Israelites, which chases the people all the way to the Red Sea. This sets the stage for one of God's greatest acts in the Old Testament, one that will serve as a foreshadowing for all future saving acts of God: the miraculous parting of the sea. With Israel backed up against the Red Sea and having no way to escape, Moses miraculously divides the waters so that the people can pass to the other side. When Pharaoh and his army try to follow the Israelites, the waters collapse upon them and they are killed. Israel is definitively freed from the Egyptians.

Coming to Know the Lord

Looking back on the strife between Moses and Pharaoh, we can see that the plagues did begin to fulfill their purpose, as some of the Egyptians at least came to see the supreme power of Israel's God. After the third plague of the gnats, Pharaoh's own magicians, for example, admit to the king, "This is the finger of God" (Ex 8:19). With the announcement of the seventh plague involving hail, some of Pharaoh's servants are described as "fearing the word of the Lord" and acting to protect their cattle and slaves from the impending punishment (Ex 9:20). After the eighth plague of the locusts, Pharaoh's servants beg him to let the people go: "Let the men go, that they may serve the Lord their God; do you not yet understand that Egypt is ruined?" (Ex 10:7).

This movement toward recognizing the supreme power of Yahweh reached a peak after the death of the firstborns, when many in Egypt joined themselves to the Israelites and followed Moses out of Egypt (Ex 12:38)—a significant turn of events that points to Israel's ultimate vocation to gather the nations into covenant with God.

The Chosen People?

Even though the people have witnessed so many miraculous manifestations of God's power, life on pilgrimage is not easy. In their hurried escape, the people have fled Egypt without adequate provisions for food or water—a significant concern for a large group of hundreds of thousands of people traveling in the desert. Nevertheless, God continues to care for their daily needs, miraculously providing them with heavenly bread (called manna) for food and the water from a rock (see Ex 16-17) as they make their way toward the Promised Land.

At Mount Sinai, God will give the Israelites the Ten Commandments and re-establish them as His covenant people. But first, the Lord reveals more of His plan for Israel—a plan that entails much more than giving them the Promised Land. God shares His vision and calling for the nation of Israel in a key passage that serves as a mission statement for God's people:

> Now therefore, if you will obey my voice and keep my
> covenant, you shall be my own possession among all
> peoples; for all the earth is mine, and you shall be to
> me a kingdom of priests and a holy nation. (Ex 19:6)

This is an important passage that sheds light on why Israel is sometimes called "the chosen people." From a modern Western perspective, this designation might seem unfair. Why would God "choose" one group of people and not another? Why does God give Israel and not the other nations Moses, the law, the prophets, and the covenant?

But this passage helps us see that God does not choose Israel *instead* of the rest of the world; He chooses Israel *for the sake of* the rest of the world.[11] God always had the entire human family in mind when He raised Israel up to be His covenantal people. From the very beginning, God intended the descendants of Abraham to be His instrument for bringing blessing to all the nations (Gn 12:3, 22:18).

At Mount Sinai, God now elaborates on this universal mission by referring to Israel as a "kingdom of priests." This indicates that God's people are called to be a great kingdom, but one with a priestly witness to the rest of the world (see Deut 4:4-7). Israel is called to act as God's representative on earth, pointing the way, like a priest, to the one, true God. This does not mean Israel was called to be like a "door-to-door" evangelist to the rest of the world. But there is an important sense in which Israel is called to witness to the truth about God and mediate His blessings to the other nations. As a kingdom of priests, Israel is to be a living prophetic witness to the world with the Lord's blessings spilling over to others who are drawn into God's covenant people. In fact, this priestly witness to the nations can be seen in God's motivation for establishing Israel as His chosen people in the preceding verse: "For all the earth is mine," God said (Ex 19:5). God's particular call for Israel has a universal scope. Why is Israel called to be a "kingdom of priests"? For the sake of the rest of the world—"for all the earth is mine," says the Lord.

This royal priestly mission also may be reflected in God's designation of Israel as his "first-born son" (Ex 4:22). Recall from the previous chapter how the father in ancient Israel possessed a kingly and priestly role in the family that was passed on to the firstborn by means of a blessing. If Israel were called God's "first-born son," it is fitting that Israel would also be seen as a kingdom of priests (Ex 19:6). Like a firstborn son in a household, Israel, as God's firstborn son in the family of nations, appropriately has a kingly and priestly mission to the other members of God's family: the other nations. Indeed, Israel is the bearer of the covenant blessings for the whole world. The question will be: How well will Israel live up to this high calling?

CHAPTER TEN
A JOURNEY THAT TESTS THE HEART
Israel's Desert Wanderings: Part One
(Exodus 24-40, Leviticus, and Numbers)

The road from Mount Sinai to the Promised Land is a bumpy one for Israel, filled with examples of heroic virtue but also fraught with many failures and lack of trust in God's love. At the end of the people's forty-year desert wanderings, Moses explains that the long journey had an important spiritual purpose: It was a period of testing. "And you shall remember all the ways which the Lord your God has led you these forty years in the wilderness, that he might humble you, *testing you to know what was in your heart*, whether you would keep his commandments or not" (Dt 8:2, emphasis added).

In the Bible, the heart is the center of a person's inner life, where one's emotions, thoughts, and actions originate. The Heavenly Father was testing His people's hearts to know whether they truly placed Him at this inner core of their being. Did they really love God above all else?

We will walk this challenging road with Israel, focusing on four key moments in the journey. In this chapter, we will look at the covenant ceremony at Mount Sinai (Ex 24) and the people's idolatry in worshiping a golden calf (Ex 32). In the next chapter, we will continue the journey with Israel as we examine how the people surprisingly reject the land God promised them and are punished to wander in the desert for forty years (Nm 14) and how, at the end of this period, a new generation of Israelites squanders an opportunity to start anew with God by falling into idolatry like their parents did at Sinai, this time with one of the gods of the people in the new land (Nm 25).

At every step of the way, we will see God testing the hearts of His people, and the people coming up short. The forty-year journey of testing will make it abundantly clear that the people have hearts that are weak, selfish, and fearful, incapable of following His commandments. But the difficult journey ends with Moses' offering hope for the future, announcing a great healing work that God will eventually accomplish: a healing of their hearts, which will cause them to walk in God's ways. This is one of the first clear foreshadowings of the healing power of God's grace in the Bible. God will solve the problem of man's sinful heart and enable His people to do what they could never do on their own. With this future spiritual healing in mind, Moses can finally say to the people something he has never been able to say confidently before: "You will love the Lord your God with all your heart." (Dt 30:6).

Test No. 1: The Heart of Worship

A crucial event in Israel's desert journey comes in Exodus 24, which tells one of the most astonishing stories in the Old Testament. After freeing the Israelites from slavery in Egypt and bringing them to Mount Sinai to receive the Ten

Commandments, God now invites the Israelite leaders up the mountain to share a meal in His divine presence.

For many Christian readers in the twenty-first century, this ritual meal may not mean much. For the ancient Israelites, however, sharing a meal had powerful symbolic connotations, expressing covenant unity and a shared life. For them, to share a meal meant that all at the table were like family. In fact, meals were so important that two enemies making a peace treaty could solidify their new covenant relationship by eating a meal together. The former enemies would leave the table as covenant partners, even using the language of family to describe their new committed friendship. Even adversaries become brothers through covenant meals (see Gn 18:26-33). Therefore, when we read about the Israelite leaders having a *meal* in God's presence, we should see this as a pivotal moment in Israel's relationship with the Lord. This ritual meal symbolizes the intimate covenant relationship God is now forging with His people.

Let's take a closer look at the structure of this covenant ceremony at Sinai, where we will discover that each of the ritual words and actions is rich in meaning. They shed light on the kind of relationship God wants with Israel and even tell us about the kind of relationship God wants to have with us today.

Bloody Sacrifice

As the leader of this ceremony, Moses first proclaims "all the words of the Lord and all the ordinances" to the people. In turn, the Israelites respond to God's commandments with faith and commitment, saying, "All the words which the Lord has spoken we will do" (Ex 24:3).

Second, Moses leads the people in a sacrificial rite that has three parts: the offering of animals, a blood ritual, and a communion meal. Each part is packed with symbolic significance.

Sacrifice: The sacrifices offered at Mount Sinai are all about God examining the hearts of His people. Will Israel's heart be truly for Yahweh or for the false gods of the pagan nations? As we saw in the last chapter, God required Israel to go into the wilderness to sacrifice animals that were associated with Egyptian deities (see Ex 8:25-27). Now that they have escaped Egypt, the Israelites have arrived at this mountain in the desert to perform the sacrificial ritual. While animal sacrifice has many levels of significance in the Old Testament, here it symbolizes a rejection of those Egyptian deities represented by those animals (see Chapter Eight) and a renewal of Israel's loyalty to Yahweh as the one, true God. Thus, in a sense, this particular sacrifice at Sinai could be seen as a ritual enactment of the First Commandment: "I am the Lord your God....You shall not have any other strange gods before me" (Ex 20:2-3).

Blood Ritual: Next, Moses performs a ritual in which he gathers the blood from the animals into basins and sprinkles half of it on the altar as an offering to God and throws the rest of it on the people. What is the significance of this strange ritual? For the ancient Israelites, blood symbolized life, and similar to sharing a meal, the sharing of blood symbolized the sharing of life and covenant union. Therefore, with half the blood being offered to God on the altar and half the blood being poured on the people, this act would symbolize a new shared life between Israel and the Lord. Now, one of the main goals of the exodus is achieved: The people of Israel have formally become one in covenant with the Almighty God.

Communion Meal: Finally, the consummation of this ceremony at Sinai is a communion meal symbolically shared between the leaders of Israel and Yahweh Himself. "Then Moses and Aaron, Nadab, and Abihu, and seventy of the leaders of Israel went up, and they saw the God of Israel…. They beheld God, and ate and drank" (Ex 24:9, 11). Because sharing a meal signifies covenant union, the fact that the Israelite leaders eat this covenant meal in God's presence symbolizes the profound relationship God forges with His people. Through this ritual, they have become sealed as God's covenant family.

Going to Sinai, Going to Mass

This ritual at Sinai is not only important for understanding a foundational moment in Israel's relationship with God; it also tells us a lot about how we as Christians are to worship the Lord today, for the specifics of this ritual at Mount Sinai reflect a divine pattern for worship. Already in the time of Moses, God establishes the basic structure for worship that He desires to be used for the rest of time. Note how, at Sinai, there is found a "liturgy of the word" and a "liturgy of sacrifice." Moses first proclaims the Word of God and then leads the people in sacrifice, a blood ritual, and a communion meal.

This pattern continues throughout the history of Israel and is fulfilled ultimately in the Eucharist that Jesus institutes. The Mass we celebrate today starts with the Liturgy of the Word and ends with a Eucharistic liturgy of *sacrifice*, in which Christ's sacrifice on the cross is made present (CCC 1362-67). We share Christ's *blood* and partake of His crucified and resurrected body in a *communion meal*. Therefore, when Catholics worship God in the Mass, they are not following the practices invented merely by some human pastor, minister, or theologian; they are participating in the divine order of worship that Jesus established at the Last Supper in the Eucharist—a liturgical structure that God foreshadowed long before, going all the way back to what He revealed at Sinai in the time of Moses.

Test No. 2: The Golden Calf

The Israelites' newly affirmed faithfulness at Sinai is about to be tested by the absence of their anointed leader. At the end of the covenant meal, the glory-cloud manifesting God's presence descends on Mount Sinai and Moses enters its midst, where he remains for forty days and forty nights, unseen by the Israelites at the base of the mountain (Ex 24:18).

Once again, God wants to see what is in their hearts. How do the Israelites fare?

> When the people saw that Moses delayed to come down from the mountain, the people gathered themselves together to Aaron, and said to him, "Up, make us gods,

who shall go before us; as for this Moses…we do not know what has become of him." (Ex 32:1)

Alone in the desert wilderness and uncertain about what happened to Moses, the people give in to their fears, and their hearts turn back to Egypt as they fall into idolatry. Although they speak about dedicating a feast to the Lord (Ex 32:5), they idolatrously worship the image of a golden bull calf, reminiscent of the Egyptian god Apis (Ex 32:4). As was typical of many pagan rituals, Israel's worship of the golden calf included debauchery, drunkenness, and sexual immorality, which is reflected by the Hebrew idiom, "The people sat down to eat and drink, and rose up to play" (Ex 32:6).

If the covenant ceremony in Exodus 24 represents a high point in Israel's relationship with God, the events surrounding the golden calf apostasy mark one of the lowest. In the covenant ceremony, the leaders ate, drank, and beheld God (Ex 24:11). Now the people eat, drink, and engage in sexual play as they worship the golden idol. So devastating was this sin for Israel that one could call it a "second fall," marking a fundamental break in Israel's relationship with God. What Adam did in the garden as an individual rebelling against God, Israel did as a nation at Sinai.

And, at least in some respects, the sin at Sinai appears graver. The people fall into idolatry *after* they have witnessed God's great love for them, liberating them from slavery with many miracles in Egypt and drawing them into intimate covenant union with Him on Sinai. Moreover, the people just accepted the First Commandment about not having other gods before Yahweh, solemnly promising to keep it (Ex 24:7). To turn to idolatry after all this is a complete rejection of the God who so lovingly rescued them and to whom they just vowed their loyalty.

'Your People'

The radical rupture in Israel's relationship with Yahweh is reflected in God's words to Moses on top of Sinai, informing him of the idolatry at the base of the mountain:

> Go down; for your people, whom you brought up out of the land of Egypt, have corrupted themselves; they have turned aside quickly out of the way which I commanded them; they have made for themselves a molten calf, and have worshipped it and sacrificed to it, and said, "These are your gods, O Israel, who brought you up out of the land of Egypt!" (Ex 32:7-8)

Notice how God seems to disown the people, no longer speaking of Israel as His own but as the people whom Moses brought out of Egypt ("*your* people, whom *you* brought up out of the land"). Yet God's words merely reflect Israel's tragic choice that day: God offered the people covenant friendship, but they reject Him and instead worship the golden calf. In doing so, they put themselves outside of the covenant union God extended to them. God's language, therefore, simply reflects Israel's decision not to live in covenant with Yahweh.

The devastating impact on Israel's relationship with the Lord is also seen when God refers to how the people "have corrupted themselves" (Ex 32:7). The Hebrew word here for "corrupted" is used in the Bible to describe a defective animal that is disqualified for sacrifice (Lv 22:25); it is also used to describe a fault that makes a man unfit for priestly service (Lv 19:27). Thus, although Israel was called to be a kingdom of priests (Ex 19:5-6), its people are now, after the golden calf apostasy, likened to a blemished animal and a disqualified priest who is unable to draw near to God's presence in the sanctuary.

The Rise of the Levitical Priesthood

This tragic sequence of events also marks the beginning of the Levitical priesthood. Up to this point, the priesthood was not limited to the Levites. In Genesis, the father performed priestly functions like building altars, offering sacrifices, and conferring blessings. In the Book of Exodus, the father's priestly function is most clearly seen in the Passover, in which it is *the father* who sacrifices the lamb and presides over the ritual in his own home (see Ex 12:3). As we saw in Genesis, these priestly roles are passed on to the firstborn son, who assumes a sacred status. In the Book of Exodus, God instructs that every firstborn son is to be consecrated to the Lord (Ex 13:2).

This special status of the firstborn sons, however, is taken away at Mount Sinai. Whether they participated in the golden calf idolatry or simply failed to stop it, the firstborn sons clearly did not step forward when Moses came down the mountain and asked, "Who is on the Lord's side?" (Ex 32:26). After this incident, the firstborn sons are likened to an unclean donkey that needs to be redeemed—bought back from service—or be killed, rather than consecrated like other animals (see Ex 34:20).[12]

When the firstborn sons lose their special priestly status, another group of people is elevated to fill it: the Levites. When Moses comes down the mountain and sees the apostasy, he calls upon faithful Israelites to put a stop to the debauchery. Only one group of people steps forward: the tribe of Levi, descendants of the great patriarch Levi, one of the sons of Jacob. In response to their heroic faithfulness that day, Moses announces their ordination, saying, "Today you have ordained yourselves for the service of the Lord" (Ex 32:29).

The next several chapters of the Bible will focus primarily on this new Levitical priesthood, which marks a fundamental shift for the Israelite people and their worship. Exodus 35-40 chronicles the construction of a new sanctuary for worship, the tabernacle. Leviticus 1-16 (commonly known as "the Priestly Code") narrates the instruction of the Levitical priesthood, their new service in the tabernacle, and their installation. And Leviticus 17-26 (commonly known as "the Holiness Code") focuses on the renewal of the people who will now be led by the new priests.

Counting Priests

The next book of the Bible, the Book of Numbers, further highlights the transfer of priestly roles from the firstborn sons to the Levites in a census of all the people. The dramatic significance of this census cannot be underestimated. Just imagine Moses gathering hundreds of thousands of people from all the tribes of Israel for the main purpose of publicly replacing the failed firstborn sons with the Levites.

That's what happens in the opening chapters of the Book of Numbers. First, Moses counts all the adult men in Israel, except those from the tribe of Levi. Second, he calls forth the faithful tribe of Levi who had defended Yahweh during the golden calf apostasy, and they number 22,000 men. Then, with all the Levites standing before Moses and in front of all the tribes of Israel, Moses calls out the disgraced firstborn sons who failed during the golden calf idolatry. There, before all their kinsmen, these unfaithful firstborn sons are separated from their brothers and replaced by the Levites in a one-to-one exchange: one Levitical priest for every demoted firstborn son.[13]

In the midst of this exchange, God explains His actions to Moses: "And you shall take the Levites for me...instead of all the first-born" (Nm 3:41). This replacement is further explained in Numbers 8:14-18, where God calls the Levites instead of the firstborn sons to serve in the sanctuary. This new Levitical order will continue until the coming of the perfect firstborn son, Jesus Christ, who will establish the new and everlasting covenant.

CHAPTER ELEVEN
GRACE IN THE END?
Israel's Desert Wanderings: Part Two
(Numbers and Deuteronomy)

So close…and yet so far! After a year's stay at Mount Sinai following the golden calf idolatry, the Israelites finally depart and head to the Promised Land (Nm 10:11). They are on the verge of receiving this great blessing God has promised the people ever since the time of Abraham. Indeed, God is prepared to give them the Land right now—but, as we will soon discover, when Israel faces its next test in the desert, their hearts are still not ready to receive this great gift. Instead of welcoming God's gift of the Land, the people shockingly reject it and are condemned to wander in the desert for forty years until they die. Then it will be up to their children as the new generation of Israelites to enter and settle the Land.

Let's turn to Numbers 13-14 to see what prevents the Israelites from entering the Promised Land at this time.

Test No. 3: Afraid to Enter the Land

In the previous chapter, we saw two ways God tested Israel's heart at Mount Sinai. Now, a third testing takes place as the people come to the edge of the Promised Land. The Lord tells

Moses to select one man from each of the twelve tribes to scout out the land of Canaan. They return bearing a mixed report. On one hand, the Land is good, flowing with milk and honey. On the other hand, they report that the people in the Land are remarkably strong and live in fortified cities. Ten of the spies view the strength of these inhabitants as an insurmountable obstacle: "We are not able to go up against the people; for they are stronger than we" (Nm 13:31). Hearing this evil report, the congregation of Israel cries out against Moses and Aaron, saying, "Would that we had died in the land of Egypt! Or would that we had died in this wilderness! Why does the Lord bring us into this land, to fall by the sword?" (Nm 14:2-3).

Outraged at the people's lack of trust in God to protect them, two of the twelve spies, Joshua and Caleb, stand up and tear their clothes, pleading with the people not to rebel against the Lord: "Do not fear the people of the land, for they are bread for us; their protection is removed from them, and the Lord is with us; do not fear them" (Nm 14:9).

But this only enrages the people all the more. They are so terrified about facing the powerful Canaanite armies that they were ready to stone Joshua and Caleb for their insistence that they follow God into this dangerous (though divinely promised) Land. At just this moment, the glory of the Lord appeared to all the people of Israel, rescuing Joshua and Caleb from the rebellious mob.

In a severe example of His justice, God grants the people what they desire. They say they don't want to enter the land;

therefore, God won't give it to them. Only Joshua and Caleb—
the two faithful spies who defended Yahweh and trusted in
His plan—will be permitted to receive God's promise (Nm
14:30). The rest of this unfaithful generation of Israelites will
be disinherited from the land and will have to wander in the
desert for forty years until they die: "Your dead bodies shall
fall in this wilderness; and of all your number, numbered from
twenty years old and upward, who have murmured against me,
not one shall come into the land where I swore that I would
make you dwell" (Nm 14:29-30). Why forty years in the desert?
God explains, "According to the number of the days in which
you spied out the land, forty days, for every day a year, you
shall bear your iniquity, forty years" (Nm 14:34).

Like Fathers, Like Sons

Israel's travel plans have taken an unexpected detour. An entire
generation of the people is condemned to wander forty years in
the desert and never enter the Promised Land. But at the end
of this period, there is hope: The older generation has passed,
and their children have now come of age. This new generation
of Israelites approaches the edge of the Promised Land that
their parents rejected and is given the opportunity to start anew
with the Lord. How will they fare? Will they learn from their
parents' mistakes and remain faithful to God?

Hopes for renewed faithfulness are quickly dashed when the
Israelites develop an association with the pagan women in the
land, which leads to their downfall. Numbers 25 tells us that
the Israelites "began to play the harlot with the daughters of

Moab" and began worshipping one of their gods, Baal of Peor
(Nm 25:2-3). This idolatry represents another dramatic break
in Israel's relationship with God—one that will be felt down
through the generations.

God's response to this new generation's idolatry is to issue a
new disciplinary law that comes to be known as Deuteronomy,
which literally means "second law."

The Second Law: A Book on the Boundary

Biblical scholar Christopher Wright describes Deuteronomy as
"a book on the boundary."[14] This certainly can be understood
geographically, since Deuteronomy was given at a place called
Beth Peor (Dt 3:29), which was only a day's journey to the
Promised Land. But this description also makes sense *morally*,
since the people of Israel have reached a critical turning point
in their relationship with God. They are about to enter the
Promised Land, whose inhabitants have built an alluring
pagan, immoral culture. Though initially hostile to Israel, these
Canaanite societies have many enticing elements that could
lead God's people astray, as was made evident by the seductive
power of the Moabite women, who lead the people quickly
into worshipping Baal of Peor. If such apostasy occurred when
the Israelites dwelt on the outskirts of these pagan cultures,
what will happen when they enter the heart of this new land?

Deuteronomy is a law that prepares the people for life
in this pagan, polytheistic society. This law is, first of all,
uncompromisingly monotheistic. Take, for example, the

monotheistic "creed" that the Israelites are to recite throughout their daily lives. Every morning and evening, and whenever they go out in the streets or sit in their homes, they are to have on their lips these solemn words professing their total allegiance to the one Lord:

> Hear, O Israel: The Lord our God is one Lord; and you shall love the Lord your God with all your heart, and with all your soul, and with all your might. (Dt 6:4-9)

In opposition to the pagan religions in the land, Deuteronomy does not simply emphasize the existence of one God but unabashedly proclaims that the one, true God is not any of the pagan deities, but the one who led the Israelites out of Egypt, entered into a special covenant relationship with them, and brought them to the Promised Land.

Deuteronomy also calls for unconditional loyalty to Yahweh in the way the people live. Faithfulness to God is more than just an intellectual conviction (that there is only one God, Yahweh); it is also a matter of the heart. The people are called to live lives that are markedly different from the pagans in the land. In Deuteronomy, perhaps more than anywhere else in the Bible, Moses emphasizes the vital necessity of steadfastly following God's commandments. Since he knows the people will face pressures to conform to the enticing pagan lifestyles around them—immoral ways of living that promise a false and fleeting happiness—Moses stresses that obedience to God's law is the only pathway to the abundant life and the true, lasting happiness that God wants to give the people:

> If you obey the commandments of the Lord your God...by loving the Lord your God, by walking in his ways, and by keeping his commandments...then you shall live and multiply, and the Lord your God will bless you in the land which you are entering to take possession of it. (Dt 30:16)

But if the people's hearts turn away from God and turn toward the pagan ways of life, they will experience the emptiness of life outside the blessing—what the Bible calls the curse.

The Two Ways

In Deuteronomy 28, Moses presents to Israel what is known as "the two ways." He challenges the people to choose between two paths: the way of life and the way of death. On one hand, if the people keep God's law, they will be blessed in the Promised Land (Dt 28:1-14). Israel will be "set high above all the nations of the earth" (Dt 28:1), and the Promised Land will be for them like a return to paradise, a new Eden. They are told that they will be blessed and fruitful with children, as Adam and Eve were told in Eden (Dt 28:4, Gn 1:26-28). The ground shall be blessed again, as well as all the work of their hands in the field (Dt 28:4, 12)—blessings that are the reversals of the curses on the ground and on man's labors after the fall (Gn 3:17-19).

But, on the other hand, if the people fail to keep the law, they will place themselves outside these wonderful blessings that God wants to give them. Instead, they will put themselves under curses, the culmination of which will be Israel's being driven from the land in exile (Dt 28:15-68). Just as Adam and Eve were expelled from the garden when they sinned, so will the Israelites be driven from the Promised Land if they break the covenant with God.

This is the choice Moses offers the people: the way of covenant faithfulness to God that leads to blessedness, and the way of infidelity that leads to death. He pleads with the people to make the right choice:

> I call heaven and earth to witness against you this day, that I have set before you life and death, blessing and curse; therefore choose life, that you and your descendants may live, loving the Lord your God, obeying his voice, and cleaving to him; for that means life to you and length of days. (Dt 30:19-20)

This challenge of the two ways applies to us, too, for we are faced with a similar choice: Every day we make decisions that lead us down the path either to the abundant life and true happiness that comes from walking in God's ways, or to the insecurity, emptiness, frustration, and disappointment that comes from not making God our priority. Right now, if you had to evaluate your own life, on which path would you say you are traveling?

Not If, But When...

Back to Israel: Which path will God's people take? Moses makes Israel's future clear: "And when all these things come upon you, the blessing and the curse, which I have set before you, and you call them to mind among the nations where the Lord your God has driven you..." (Dt 30:1). These are ominous words. Notice how Moses does not say "*if* all these things come upon you," but "*when*." In other words, Moses knows Israel is going to be unfaithful to the covenant. He foretells that Israel will experience some of the blessings in the land, but, in the end, the people will break the covenant and the curses will fall upon them. They will lose the land and be scattered among the nations in exile.

These curses will bring God's people face to face with their own brokenness, humbly standing before the Lord and crying out for mercy. One theological reflection we could draw out of the Book of Deuteronomy is how the law helps the people recognize their weakness and beg for God's help and mercy. The Ten Commandments were given at Mount Sinai, but the Israelites' forty years in the desert have made it evident that they do not yet have the heart to keep God's commands. As the next several books of the Bible will reveal, their future life in the Promised Land will make their weakness all the more evident. God's people might possess the law—so they *know* what is good—but they do not seem to have the ability to keep it.

This points to one important purpose of the law: It reveals both the good that we should do and our utter inability to live it out. The Lord's commandments, therefore, make it abundantly clear how much we need God's grace to fulfill the law, and it humbles us so that we are more inclined to call out to the Lord for help. As St. Augustine explained in *The Spirit and the Letter*,

"The law was given so that grace might be sought; grace was given so that the law might be fulfilled."

Circumcision of Heart

This healing power of grace is foreshadowed in the same passage of Deuteronomy that offers a bleak forecast about Israel's future in exile. In this condition of exiled suffering, the Israelites will turn their hearts to God and God will rescue them, bringing them back to the land:

> And when all these things come upon you, the blessing and the curse, which I have set before you, and you call them to mind among all the nations where the Lord your God has driven you, and return to the Lord your God, you and your children, and obey his voice in all that I command you this day, with all your heart and with all your soul; then the Lord your God will restore your fortunes, and have compassion upon you, and he will gather you again from all the peoples. (Dt 30:1-3)

Furthermore, Moses foretells how God will accomplish an even *greater* act of salvation for the Israelites than rescuing them from their enemies. God will perform a profound work in their own hearts, empowering them to finally fulfill the law.

> And the Lord your God will circumcise your heart and the heart of your offspring, so that you will love the Lord your God with all your heart and with all your soul, that you may live.... And you shall again obey

the voice of the Lord, and keep all his commandments. (Dt. 30:6, 8)

In these verses, we encounter one of the most important prophecies in the Bible so far about the kind of salvation that God wants to work in our lives. God doesn't want merely obedient servants who follow His commandments; ultimately, He wants sons and daughters who love Him. He doesn't just want external obedience—simply doing what is right; like a lover, he wants our hearts. The people of Israel have demonstrated that their hearts are weak, selfish, fearful, and incapable of remaining faithful to the Lord. This is not a problem specific to Israel; not one of us, by our own power, is capable of loving God the way we ought. But Moses announces that God will heal their wounded hearts and give His people the ability to do what they could not do on their own. This transformation of their hearts will cause them to walk in God's ways, so much so that Moses can finally say to them, "You will love the Lord your God with all your heart."

This is the ultimate goal for God's dealings with Israel throughout the Exodus story. God wants to free His people not only from slavery in Egypt, but from slavery to sin. He wants to take them through "an internal exodus" in which their hearts are healed and they are transformed by His love. All this, of course, foreshadows the work that Jesus Christ will accomplish through His death, resurrection, and sending "the Spirit into our hearts," so that, "led by the Spirit," we can finally live as sons and daughters of God, faithfully loving and serving Him as our heavenly Father (Rom 8:13-15, Gal 4:6).

CHAPTER TWELVE
A LAND WITHOUT A LEADER
Israel's Downward Spiral, from Joshua to Samson
(Joshua and Judges)

After the death of Moses, we encounter two key figures in the next two books of the Bible who represent different kinds of leaders for Israel in the Promised Land—leaders who will either inspire the nation to godly living or drag the people down because of their own personal weaknesses.

At one end of the spectrum, Joshua stands out as the courageous leader who is committed to God's covenant, challenges the people spiritually, and encourages them to live a more godly life. On the other end of the spectrum, Samson is a failed leader who is a slave to his passions. Though endowed with unique gifts, he does not have the inner moral strength to use those gifts for good. Lacking self-control, Samson gives in to his anger, his stomach, and his sexual appetites, selfishly using his gifts to pursue pleasure for himself instead of carrying out his mission to help others and rescue the Israelites from their oppressors.

As salvation history moves to its next phase in the Promised Land, the stories of Joshua and Samson remind us that real strength lies not in muscles, wealth, sex, or power, but deep within the soul that remains faithful to God.

The Book of Joshua: Entering the Land

Let's begin by considering the exemplary leadership of Joshua. After Moses dies, the governance of Israel now passes on to this man, who had been Moses' faithful servant throughout the desert wanderings. God first assures Joshua of His presence, calling him to be "strong and courageous" and careful to follow the law that Moses had given, as he is about to lead the people into the Promised Land (Jos 1:5-9). Joshua was one of the few who had faith in God's promises when the Israelites rebelled out of fear that God would not protect them, after which they were forced to wander the desert for forty years until they perished. At last, Joshua stands at the Jordan River, ready to lead the people into that same land that their parents had rejected.

By means of a miracle reminiscent of the parting of the Red Sea, Joshua parts the Jordan River, and the Israelites pass over into the Promised Land on dry ground (Jos 4). Their first significant action is to head to the fortified city of Jericho, where God demonstrates how the Israelites will possess the land originally promised to their forefather Abraham: not by military might alone, but by divine intervention.

Jericho is often noted for its very large walls. Scripture itself says that some people even had their homes built *inside* the walls (Jos 2:15). But this heavily fortified city ends up falling not through weapons but through worship, as the Levites guide the nation in a procession around Jericho, with the Ark of the Covenant leading the way. They do this for seven consecutive days, culminating with trumpet blasts and shouts from the people—and miraculously, the walls tumble down without the use of a single weapon. The message of this first victory in the Promised Land is clear: Israel will come to possess the land not through its own machinations or military might, but through the intervention and protection of the Lord.

Covenant Renewal at Shechem

The rest of the Book of Joshua chronicles the initial settling of the Promised Land until, at the end of his life, Joshua gathers the people one last time at Shechem. This place is significant, for it was the first place in the land of Canaan where Abraham had built an altar to worship God, marking out the land God gave to him and his descendants (Gn 12:6). Now, centuries later, Joshua gathers the people together and calls them to worship the one, true God, just as their father Abraham had done at this same sacred place.

However, there is one problem Joshua needs to address first: Idolatry is still plaguing the people. This new generation of Israelites has fallen into the same sin as the generation before, bringing Egypt's idolatry into the Promised Land. Joshua confronts the people and calls them to renounce their idolatry once and for all, saying, "Now therefore fear the Lord, and serve Him in sincerity and in faithfulness; put away the gods which your fathers served beyond the River, and in Egypt, and serve the Lord" (Jos 24:14).

Joshua stands here as a new Moses. Just as Moses, near the end of his life, challenged the people to choose between the way of obedience that leads to life and the way of covenant infidelity that leads to death, so too does Joshua, near the end of *his* days, force the people to make a choice between the pagan gods and Yahweh. He says to them, "Choose this day whom you will serve," and he leads the people with his own pledge of fidelity: "As for me and my house, we will serve the Lord" (Jos 24:15).

Joshua's challenge was effective: The Scriptures tell us, "And Israel served the Lord all the days of Joshua, and all the days of the elders who outlived Joshua and had known all the work which the Lord did for Israel" (Jos 24:31).

The Book of Judges: The Downward Spiral

The Book of Judges, however, opens up with a dramatic shift in Israel's history. For two generations, the people have flourished under the godly leadership of Moses and Joshua—true spiritual leaders, calling the people to faithfulness. But after Joshua's death, Israel languishes without strong leaders who challenge them to walk in the Lord's ways. The Second Chapter of Judges announces the harmful results of this leadership vacuum: "There arose another generation...who did not know the Lord" and began to serve other gods from the nations around them (Jgs 2:10-12).

To feel the full force of this statement, recall how the fundamental purpose of the exodus from Egypt was to liberate Israelites so that they could *know* the Lord—to live in covenant with Him—and to *serve* Him, which means to worship him (see Ex 4:22). The fact that this next generation no longer even *knows* the Lord and is *serving* other gods represents a reversal of the exodus. Although God has redeemed (literally, "bought back") the Israelites from the Egyptians (Ex 6:6, 15:13), He now "sold them into the power of their enemies round about" (Jgs 2:14). This highlights the critical importance of handing on the faith: No matter how faithful one generation is, there will be a cultural crisis if the faith is not passed on to the next generation.

In the Book of Judges, we come face to face with the Israelites' spiritual amnesia: they no longer even know the Lord. Furthermore, they have forgotten who they are and how they need to live as God's chosen people.

This is the beginning of a catastrophic cycle that will enslave Israel for more than 300 years. Seven times in the Book of Judges, Israel falls into the following pattern of sin, slavery, supplication, and salvation:

- *Sin*: First, the people forget the Lord and fall into sin by serving foreign gods.
- *Slavery:* Second, their punishment is to be enslaved by foreign nations that oppress them.
- *Supplication:* In their distress, they cry out to God in supplication.
- *Salvation:* God sends them a judge to save them from their enemies—at least, until they fall back into sin and repeat the cycle.

The fact that this cycle of sin repeats over and over again demonstrates that the judges whom God sends to rescue the people do not have a lasting spiritual impact. Some may successfully free the people from their enemies, but even they do not seem to challenge the people to turn away from their sins. Moreover, many judges are themselves corrupt, leading the people away from God's law.

Strength Is More than Physical

This fact is demonstrated most clearly in the life of the famous judge Samson. Samson embodies both the call and the weakness of God's people. He was endowed with extraordinary gifts of strength and a mission to liberate Israel from their current oppressors, the Philistines. Moreover, an angel revealed to his parents that he was to be consecrated to the Lord as a Nazirite. Nazirites were Israelite men and women who were set apart for special service to the Lord. They expressed their consecration by vowing to never consume alcohol, cut their hair, or come in close contact with a corpse (Jgs 13:4-5, Nm 6:1-8).

Though Samson was called to do great things for the Lord, he failed to carry out his mission. Instead of liberating Israel from the Philistines, he fell into their pagan ways, marrying a pagan woman, getting drunk, murdering in vengeance, and taking a prostitute. In the end, he died as one of their prisoners. Samson is a man who gives in to his passions for food, drink, and sex. Though physically strong, he was not strong in virtue. His moral weakness leads him to break his three Nazirite vows.

First, Samson sees a swarm of bees and honey inside the carcass of a lion. He was so desperate for the honey that he scrapes it out of the carcass with his hands and eats it—even though this violates his vow to avoid corpses (Jgs 14:8-9).

Second, the Bible tells us that Samson goes to the vineyards of Timnah and has a feast there, "for so the young men used to do" (Jgs 14:10). The word for feast (*mishteh*) implies a drinking bout. Samson thus violates his second vow of a Nazarite, that of abstaining from wine or strong drink.

Third, when the seductive Philistine woman Delilah pleads with him day after day to reveal the secret of his strength, Samson finally gives in and tells her, "A razor has never come upon my head for I have been a Nazirite to God from my mother's womb. If I be shaved, then my strength will leave me, and I shall become weak, and be like any other man" (Jgs 16:18). With this knowledge, Delilah has Samson's head shaved while he is sleeping, and his third vow is broken. The strength of the Lord immediately leaves him, and he is captured by the Philistines, who gouge out his eyes.

Samson and Delilah's very names sum up the story of this tragic judge: The name Samson is connected with the Hebrew word *shemesh* (which means sun) and can be translated "sun child."[15] Delilah's name literally means "lady of the night." Samson was called to do great things for Israel and for the Lord—in a sense, to be a light for God's people. But in the end, this "sun child" of Israel is eclipsed by a Philistine "lady of the night."

The life of Samson embodies the history of Israel in the period of the judges. Israel was called uniquely among all the nations to serve the Lord in this Promised Land, but like Samson, the Israelites intermarry with the pagans and live more like the people around them than as sons and daughters set apart for the Lord. Enticed by the pagan ways of life around them, the Israelites break covenant with God and fall into greed, murder, sexual immorality, and idolatry, all culminating in a great civil war.

The result of this spiritual death spiral can be seen in the final verse of the Book of Judges: "In those days there was no king of Israel; every man did what was right in his own eyes" (Jgs 21:25). With no spiritual leader like Joshua to lead them and challenge them, the people fall deeper and deeper into the slavery of sin.

CHAPTER THIRTEEN
A KING AFTER GOD'S OWN HEART
Saul, David, and the Rise of the Kingdom
(1 Samuel and 2 Samuel)

The First Book of Samuel begins with Israel beaten down and exhausted by the sins and failures of its leaders. The people turn to the last of their judges, a man named Samuel, and ask him for a king. This, in itself, is a noble request: All the way back in Genesis, God had promised Abraham that kings would eventually come from his descendants. Unfortunately, the people don't ask for a king who would be a spiritual leader like Moses and Joshua; rather, they want a king "like all the nations" (1 Sm 8:5). God concedes and gives them the kind of king they desire: Saul.

From a worldly perspective, Saul is the ideal king. He is tall, handsome, wealthy, popular, and great on the battlefield—a natural leader. What Saul is not, however, is a man after the Lord's own heart. He is proud and vain, wanting to be liked more than to lead the people to what is best for them. He is the kind of leader who is always worried about public opinion and what others think of him. Despite his significant military achievements, he is incapable of securing the Promised Land for Israel. In the end, he disobeys one of God's commands because he feared that, if he followed it, the people would think less of him (1 Sm 13:8-12, 15:24). God announces that He will take away Saul's kingship, because he put his desire to be accepted by others over obedience to God's law (1 Sm 13:13-14, 15:26-28).

Passing over Saul, the Lord has Samuel anoint a new king who will be a man after the Lord's own heart (1 Sm 13:14). His name is David, and he is nothing like his predecessor. He is a mere youth, too young to be a soldier. His only experience has been shepherding sheep while his brothers were off at war. Yet this is the man the Lord commands Samuel to anoint, telling him, "The Lord sees not as man sees; man looks on the outward appearance, but the Lord looks on the heart" (1 Sm 16:7).

In reality, David was much more than a shepherd boy. The Scriptures tell us that, despite his diminutive size, he has a warrior's heart. While he was alone tending sheep, he defended his flock by killing lions and bears that tried to attack them (see 1 Sm 17:36). His faithfulness eventually leads David to the battlefield when he brings food and supplies to his brothers, who are supposed to be fighting for Israel on the front lines against the Philistines. What he finds there, however, surprises him: The Israelites are in a standoff with their enemies, with the champion of the Philistines, Goliath, having challenged any Israelite to engage him in battle.

What most surprises David is that, for forty days, no Israelite had stepped forward. Seeing this as a clear battle between God's people and the pagans, David asks, "Who is this uncircumcised Philistine, that he should defy the armies of the living God?" (1

Sm 17:26). David confidently trusts that the Lord will defeat the enemy and does what no other man in Israel's camp was willing to do: He goes out to meet Goliath. With a bold faith reminiscent of Joshua, David says, "You come to me with sword and with a spear and with a javelin; but I come to you in the name of the Lord of hosts, the God of the armies of Israel, whom you have defied" (1 Sm 17:45).

Before he uses his famous slingshot, David says: "This day the Lord will deliver you into my hand...that all the earth may know that there is a God in Israel, and that all this assembly may know that the Lord saves not with sword and spear; for the battle is the Lord's and he will give you into our hand" (1 Sm 17:47).

Remember that *knowing* the Lord was a key goal of the Exodus story and that, ever since the period of the judges, Israel had failed to keep covenant with God. Now, with David, Israel finally has an emerging spiritual leader who challenges the people to *know* the Lord once again.

Second Book of Samuel: Israel Becomes a Great Dynasty

Eventually, King Saul dies in battle, and all the tribes of Israel gather around David to enter into covenant with him as their new king (2 Sm 5:1-4). David's first move as king is to capture the city of Jerusalem, an event that sets the stage for a pivotal moment in David's life and in Israel's history. With this last Canaanite stronghold in the Promised Land finally defeated, the Israelites can rest from their enemies about them (2 Sm

7:1). The people can now live secure in the land that was promised to Abraham back in Genesis 12—the land to which Israel was led by Moses and Joshua, and which it now finally possesses in tranquility, thanks to David.

This sparks David to do something he had never done before. David had won many military victories in his lifetime, but he had never called for the Ark of the Covenant to be transferred to those places. Yet in 2 Samuel 6, David sends for the Ark to be permanently stationed in Jerusalem, which will soon become the home of a central sanctuary for God's people.

Why does he do this? David is a faithful Israelite, and the narrative of salvation history has never been far from his mind. He recognizes in these dramatic events the fulfillment of God's promises. He knows that, when the Israelites find rest, they are to establish a central sanctuary in the land (Dt 12:9-11). With Israel finally secure, it is time to build a house for the Lord—in other words, a temple for the Ark.

But God has other plans: The Lord wants to build *David* a house. The prophet Nathan announces to David: "Thus says the Lord: 'Would you build me a house to dwell in?... Moreover the Lord declares to you that the Lord will make you a house'" (2 Sm 7:5, 11).

The Hebrew word for house (*bayit*) here has three meanings. It can refer to a son or an heir; a kingdom or dynasty; or an actual building, a home.[16] God seems to have in mind all three levels of meaning, as He goes on to tell David,

> I will raise up your offspring after you, who shall come
> forth from your body, and I will establish his kingdom.
> He shall build a house for my name, and I will establish
> the throne of his kingdom forever. I will be his father,
> and he shall be my son. (2 Sm 7:12-13)

Notice how all three meanings of *bayit* come into play here.
God speaks of an actual "offspring," a son that will come to
David, and this son will be given a dynasty—a "kingdom"
and a "throne" forever. Finally, this son will build an actual
building, a "house" for God's name—in other words, a temple.

Here, David is given much more than a kingdom, like Saul; he
is promised an everlasting dynasty, where his descendants will
rule forever.

For centuries, Israel had been longing for the second great
promise God made to Abraham—a great name or a dynastic
line of kings (Gn 12:2; 17:6, 16)—to be fulfilled. When David
hears that God is going to make for *him* a great name (2 Sm
7:9) and give *him* a never-ending kingdom, he realizes that this
second promise is being fulfilled in *him*! Overwhelmed with
emotion, David thus exclaims: "Who am I, O Lord God, and
what is my house, that thou hast brought me thus far?" (2
Sm 7:18). In awe, David realizes that the great dynasty God
promised more than one thousand years ago is being given to
his own household.

At this moment, David stands at a crucial turning point in the
history of the world. As king of this new dynasty, David realizes

that Israel is positioned to move toward the fulfillment of her ultimate calling: to be a source of blessing for every family on earth—the third and final promise given to Abraham. This sheds light on an intriguing statement David then makes to God: "Thou hast shown me law for humanity" (2 Sm 7:19). [17] The significance of this statement is often missed due to awkward translations. The Hebrew text of this verse (*wasoth torath ha'adam*) includes the Hebrew word for *torah*, the covenant law, and the Hebrew word for humanity (or *adam*). Hence, David seems to understand that law for humanity is being entrusted to him. Yet some might wonder why David would say he was given law *for humankind*: David is just the king over Israel, not the ruler over the human race. He may possess law for Israel, but why would he say that God has shown him the law for the human family?

The answer has to do with Israel's mission. With the land and kingdom firmly in place, Israel is finally poised to become the great kingdom of priests that it was always meant to be (see Ex 19:6). As the shepherd of the dynasty that is meant to bear witness to the truth about God, David realizes that the law entrusted to him is meant not just for Israel; it has profound implications for the rest of the world. Hence, he can make a statement no one else in the Bible had ever said before: He proclaims that God has shown him law for mankind.

CHAPTER FOURTEEN
A KINGDOM DIVIDED AGAINST ITSELF
From Dynasty to Exile
(1 Kings, 2 Kings, and Daniel)

"It was the best of times, it was the worst of times." This opening line from Charles Dickens' *A Tale of Two Cities* could certainly be used to describe the rise and fall of the Davidic monarchy. We can see this right from the dynasty's beginnings. On one hand, the combined reigns of David and Solomon represent a high point in Israel's history: Israel experiences prosperity, territorial expansion, and the conversion of many nations that turn to their king to hear the wisdom of God. But on the other hand, the cancerous effects of sin still lurk in the background of these men's lives and end up undermining God's covenantal kingdom.

Near the end of his life, David crowns Solomon as his successor in the dynastic kingdom. The covenantal protection God promised to David will pass on to Solomon and all his royal heirs. However, the kingdom he entrusts to Solomon has been wounded by David's own sins. In 2 Samuel 11, David commits adultery with Bathsheba and orders the murder of her husband, Uriah. Though David sincerely repented (2 Sm 12:13; *cf.* Ps 51) and was indeed forgiven by the Lord, we will see how the effects of his sins will continue to haunt the dynasty in the next generation and all the way up to the coming of Christ.

Let's look at how the short-lived glory of Israel is embodied in the life of David's first heir, King Solomon.

Solomon Prefiguring Christ

Solomon starts off as a noble and faithful king who takes Israel to its highest point in its history. When God offers to bless him in any way he chooses, Solomon asks for something that wouldn't simply serve himself but would help him rule the people well: He asks for the gift of wisdom. Solomon also carried out his father's wishes to build the Lord's house, spending seven years constructing the temple and then leading his people in worship at the ceremonial dedication of this new central sanctuary.

Solomon's greatness is seen most vividly in his international influence, leading even some from the pagan nations to the wisdom of God. The First Book of Kings highlights how many gentile kings covenant themselves to Solomon's kingdom because they want to learn from his divinely given wisdom: "And men came from all peoples to hear the wisdom of Solomon, and from all the kings of the earth, who had heard of his wisdom" (1 Kgs 4:34). For a brief period, we see in Solomon the fulfillment of what David had said about the dynasty: that it would be a vehicle for the law for humanity (2 Sm 7:19).

In these ways, Solomon prefigures Jesus Christ. He is the son of David and king of Israel; he is known for his divine wisdom and for being the temple builder; and his kingdom has international influence. His life is a foreshadowing of Jesus, who is the ultimate son of David and the king who fulfills all the promises made to David's dynasty. Like Solomon, Jesus is known for His great wisdom and is the one who builds the new temple in His body (Jn 2); and it is Christ's kingdom that ultimately fulfills Israel's worldwide mission, extending God's reign over all the earth.

The Fall of Solomon

However, while Solomon takes Israel to its highest glory, he also drags the nation down to one of the lowest points in its history. How did such a good, wise, and successful king fall so quickly and so hard? In the shadow of Solomon's great triumphs lurk the secrets that lead to the unraveling of his kingdom.

The First Book of Kings shows how Solomon spent seven years building the temple in Jerusalem (1 Kgs 6:38). But in the very next verse, the narrative tells us Solomon spent thirteen years building his *own* palace, a building that was almost four times larger than the Lord's temple. While Solomon appeared to love and worship God, he began to use his wisdom and authority to serve his own selfish interests rather than God and the people.

The Scriptures provided the future kings of Israel clear guidance on how to use their authority and avoid certain traps that ensnared other worldly leaders. Deuteronomy 17 warns kings not to use their authority to serve themselves in three specific ways—by building up their military might, multiplying their wives, or increasing wealth for themselves.

Unlike David, Solomon gradually becomes openly defiant of God's word when he breaks all three of these stipulations. First, Solomon begins using his authority to gather 1,400 chariots and 12,000 horsemen—a violation of the first command for the king (1 Kgs 10:26).

Second, Solomon uses his royal position to build up a large harem of 700 wives and 300 concubines, many of whom were pagans who seduced Solomon into idolatry. We are told that "his wives turned away his heart after their gods" (1 Kgs 11:4) and that Solomon built temples to the pagan deities and "did what was evil in the sight of the Lord" (1 Kgs 11:4-8).

Third, Solomon used his royal position to increase his own wealth to excessive proportions. In addition to other revenues from foreigners, Solomon receives in one year 666 talents of gold—a number symbolizing the epitome of evil.[18] While Solomon prefigures Christ in his kingship, his wisdom, and his construction of the new temple, he also becomes an anti-Christ figure in his self-indulgence and rejection of the ways of the one, true God. Indeed, Solomon's three-fold temptation toward money, sex, and power will remain formidable challenges to all who seek to overcome the world and follow the Lord.

As a result of Solomon's sinfulness, God curses the dynasty and announces that the kingdom will become divided. "I will surely tear the kingdom from you and will give it to your servant. Yet for the sake of David your father I will not do it in your days, but I will tear it out of the hand of your son" (1 Kgs 11:11-12). This prophecy is carried out in the life of his heir, Rehoboam.

The events that unfold in Rehoboam's reign fundamentally alter the rest of Israel's history. The united kingdom of the twelve tribes of Israel will be divided into two warring monarchies, with brothers battling brothers, until the two separate nations are brought to ruin.

Divided Kingdom

In a misguided effort to consolidate his power, the new king, Rehoboam, decides to raise the already oppressive taxes in the land (1 Kgs 12:1-16). This sparks the rebellion of the ten northern tribes under their self-appointed leader, Jeroboam, splitting the kingdom into two. In the north, the ten tribes gather to form a newly aligned kingdom around Jeroboam and arrogate to themselves the name "Israel." In the south, the remaining tribes of Judah and Benjamin, along with the priestly Levites, form the Kingdom of Judah.

Recognizing the distinction between these two separated kingdoms is key to understanding the rest of the Old Testament. From now on, whenever "Israel" is mentioned, it is often a reference to the ten northern tribes that are in rebellion with the Davidic dynasty. On the other hand, references to "Judah" call to mind those people in union with the divinely appointed royal sons of David.

The rebellion of the northern tribes is more than a political division. Their split quickly turns to apostasy, as the ten northern tribes separate from the central sanctuary of the temple in Jerusalem and establish their own cities of worship in Bethel and Dan. They also separate from the divinely appointed Levitical priesthood, as Jeroboam appoints his own "priests" to serve at these unsanctioned shrines (1 Kgs 13:33-34). Finally, Jeroboam, who spent his younger years in Egypt, imports idolatrous Egyptian practices into his realm as he leads his people to worship two golden calves, reminiscent of Israel's idolatry at Mount Sinai (1 Kgs 12:28).

The northern kingdom thus rebels not just against the Davidic kings but against God's covenantal plan for the Davidic dynasty, the Levitical priesthood, and the temple in Jerusalem. Meanwhile, the people there rebel against God Himself as they start worshiping false deities. Because of their unfaithfulness, the northern kingdom does not survive for long. It begins a quick downward spiral of civil strife, sin, and rebellion against God that culminates in the nation's destruction. In 722 B.C., the Assyrians invade the region and send many people from the northern tribes into exile, while they resettle the land with five pagan nations (2 Kgs 17). The effect of this imposed assimilation with the pagans will drive the northern tribes even further away from their Davidic king and their covenant with God.

Trouble in the South

In the southern kingdom of Judah, the kings are not that much better, as almost all of them either lead the people into idolatry or fail to curb the idolatrous practices of their wicked predecessors. Their continued failure to lead the people spiritually allows the kingdom to fall into covenant disobedience, triggering the curses of Deuteronomy 28. As Moses foretold in that passage, Israel's infidelity to God's covenant will lead them into exile: In 586 B.C., the Babylonians attack Jerusalem, burn the temple to the ground, and lead all but the poorest and weakest of the Jews into exile, forcing them to be slaves in Babylon.

Though suffering in a foreign land, Israel receives some consolation from the prophets who remind the people that God has not abandoned them and that, one day, God will rescue them from their enemies and provide a definitive restoration of the Davidic kingdom.

One such prophecy comes from a Jewish youth who grew up in the Babylonian exile: the prophet Daniel. The Babylonian king has a strange dream about a large statue with the head made of gold, its breasts and arms of silver, its belly and thighs of bronze, its legs of iron, and its feet partly of iron and partly of clay. The king then saw a stone cut without human hands that struck the statue and destroyed it. But the stone became a great mountain and filled the entire earth (Dn 2:31-35).

Daniel was given insight from God to interpret the dream. He explains that the four parts of the statue represent a series of four pagan kingdoms that will dominate the region and oppress the Jews. In the classical interpretation of this prophecy, the first part, the head of gold, represents the current world power, Babylon (Dn 2:38). The next three parts of the statue represent three future kingdoms that rule the region over the next several centuries: the Medo-Persian kingdom that ruled from 539 to 331 B.C.; the Greeks, who ruled over the land from 331 to 63 B.C.; and the Roman Empire, who ruled the Jews from 63 B.C. to the time of Christ.

At the climax of Daniel's interpretation, he announces that, in the days of that fourth and most fierce kingdom (which is later shown to be Rome), God himself will establish His own kingdom, which will never end. The rock that smashes the statue and becomes a great world-filling mountain represents the worldwide kingdom God will establish in those days, while the destruction of the statue symbolizes God's judgment upon those pagan oppressors. "And in the days of those kings the God of heaven will set up a kingdom which shall never be destroyed.... It shall break in pieces all these kingdoms and bring them to an end, and it shall stand forever" (Dn 2:44).

For Daniel and the Jews in exile, this prophecy would inspire great hope. Even though they are suffering as slaves in Babylon, God has not forgotten His promise about the Davidic kingdom. A new king will come who will establish it forever.

Seventy Weeks of Years

The Book of Daniel not only provides a roadmap for the rest of Israel's history up to the time of Christ; it also offers a timetable.

The Jews spend about seventy years in Babylon. Near the end of that exile, the angel Gabriel announces to Daniel that, while the Jews will soon return to Jerusalem, the full restoration of the kingdom will come much further in the future. Gabriel announces that this process will take "seventy weeks of years"

(Dn 9:24). Following seventy years of exile, there will be seven times seventy years—"seventy weeks of years"—before the restoration will occur and a new anointed king will come.

In other words, after having waited seventy years in Babylon, God's people are told that they will now have to wait seven times this long—some 490 years—before the full restoration of Israel and the coming of the great messiah. At the end of this period, sin will be atoned for, all prophecy will be fulfilled, and everlasting righteousness will be established (Dn 9:24). An anointed one (a king) will be set apart and will establish a worldwide covenant with the many nations (see Dn 9:26-27).

This may help explain why, some 490 years later—precisely when the Jews are suffering under the oppression of the fourth pagan nation, the Romans—many in Israel are longing for the coming of the messiah and of God's kingdom. It also sheds light on why many Jews responded so enthusiastically to John the Baptist's message: "Repent, for the kingdom of heaven is at hand!" (Mt 3:2).

CHAPTER FIFTEEN
THE CLIMAX OF THE COVENANT
Jesus and the Church
(The Gospels and Acts of the Apostles)

It's difficult to imagine the sense of despair—and also hope—many Jews must have experienced in the first century A.D. For most of the last 500 years, God's people had been without a Davidic king, oppressed by various foreign powers and suffering like exiles in their own land. The Roman Empire represented the latest and fiercest of the regimes oppressing the Jewish people. Under the unprecedented force of Roman domination, violence, and taxation the Jewish people were, on many levels, suffering as never before.

Nevertheless, against this backdrop of pain and misery, their expectation and desire for a restored kingdom and a messianic savior were reaching a fevered pitch.

It is in the midst of this drama that a strange figure appears in the desert, clothed only in animal skins and eating insects and wild honey. His name is John, and he stands at the Jordan River, telling the people, "Repent!" Just as Joshua led the people through the wilderness to this very river and into the Promised Land centuries ago at the culmination of the first exodus, so now John leads the people to these same waters and invites them to a new and even greater exodus: an interior journey away from sin. He proclaims, "Repent, for the kingdom of heaven is at hand" (Mt 3:2).

The Old Testament prophets foretold that God would one day come to rescue His people from their oppressors and restore the great Davidic kingdom. They also depicted that restoration of Israel as a new exodus. It's no wonder, then, that John's message in the desert by the Jordan River (recalling the climax of the Exodus story) and his announcement about a great kingdom dawning (stirring the hopes about a future Davidic king) drew a lot of attention. Large crowds went out to follow him, hoping that the long-expected kingdom would soon arrive.

Then, one day, it finally happens: A young and unknown descendant of David named Jesus comes out to join this movement in the wilderness. He goes to John and asks to be baptized. As He rises from the waters, the Spirit of God descends upon Him, and a heavenly voice speaks the words that signal His true identity: "This is my beloved Son, with whom I am well pleased" (Mt 3:17). Indeed, now that Jesus is present, the kingdom of heaven *is* truly at hand.

The King

At the heart of Jesus' public ministry, we find more than abstract principles about ethics or salvation. As king, Jesus' mission is to restore the kingdom of David. Everywhere He goes, He preaches "the gospel of the kingdom" (Mt 4:23), which attracts people from all around the land (Mt 4:25). His famous Sermon on the Mount begins and ends with a message about the kingdom. Through His powerful healings, He is recognized as "the son of David," the true king of the Jews. Much of His preaching and many of His parables elaborate upon this kingdom with various images: It is like a field, a treasure, a mustard seed, a pearl of great price. Clearly, Jesus is claiming to usher in a great kingdom. In the first-century Jewish context, practically everyone would understand that kingdom to be the promised restoration of the kingdom of David.

At a key turning point in His public ministry, Jesus calls His disciples to recognize that the central issue of this kingdom is His very identity. He asks the disciples, "Who do you say that I am?" In response, Peter declares, "You are the Christ, the Son of the living God" (Mt 16:16). The term "Christ" refers to the anointed messiah king whom the prophets foretold.

Peter is the first to refer explicitly to Jesus as the Christ, the messiah. In response to Peter's faith, Jesus gives him the keys of His kingdom:

> And I tell you, you are Peter, and on this rock I will build my Church, and the powers of death shall not prevail against it. I will give you the keys of the kingdom of heaven, and whatever you bind on earth shall be bound in heaven, and whatever you loose on earth shall be loosed in heaven. (Mt 16:18-19)

These keys of the kingdom symbolically represent one of the most important offices in the Davidic kingdom: the head of the royal household. In the Davidic dynasty of old, the king had a prime minister–like official who was vested with the king's authority and who governed the day-to-day affairs of the kingdom. His office was symbolized by "the key of the house of David" (Is 22:22). With this background in mind, it becomes clear that, when Jesus the king gives Peter the keys of the kingdom, He is setting Peter up as the prime minister in the kingdom that He is establishing. It is no surprise that the Catholic Church sees this passage as shedding light on the papacy, since it highlights the important leadership role Jesus gave to Peter (and those who succeed him in this office of prime minister) over the Church Christ founded.

Climax of the Covenant

Jesus' kingdom will be established in a paradoxical manner. Despite His many Jewish followers, the rulers of the Jews reject Him, handing Him over to the Romans to be crucified. Yet it is through His death on that cross and His resurrection on the third day that Jesus saves His people and establishes the never-ending kingdom.

How does this occur? Consider how all the covenants we have been studying—from Adam, Noah, and Abraham to Moses and David—converge on the cross and find their fulfillment there, shedding light on the meaning of Christ's atoning sacrifice.

Jesus, as the new Adam, finds Himself in a garden (the Garden of Gethsemane) tested by the devil, but He proves to be a faithful Son (whereas Adam was unfaithful). He bore Adam's curses—sweat, thorns, and death (Gn 3:18-19)—by sweating blood, being crowned with thorns, and dying on the cross (see Chapter One).

Like Noah, Jesus is a faithful son of Adam in the midst of a corrupt world. Like Noah, He offers salvation to His household, the family of God. Noah's salvation came through the ark, which the Church Fathers saw as prefiguring the Church. Just as God used the ark to save Noah's family from the flood, so does Christ save all humanity from sin through the Church He established by His death and resurrection (see Chapter Two and CCC 845).

Like Abraham's only beloved son Isaac, Jesus, as the heavenly Father's only beloved son, travels on a donkey to the ancient Mount Moriah, now in the city of Jerusalem, and bears the wood of sacrifice to Calvary in order to offer himself as a voluntary victim to atone for our sins and bring blessing to the entire world (see Chapter Four).

Like Moses, who began the exodus from Egypt with the Passover, Jesus begins His passion—the work of the new exodus—with the Passover meal at the Last Supper. Just as the first Passover lambs were slain to spare the firstborn Israelites in Egypt, so Jesus is sacrificed on the cross as the new Passover lamb, offering redemption to all humanity. And as the Passover was not just a sacrifice but a meal, all who participate in this new Passover are called to consume the flesh of the sacrificial lamb, Jesus Christ, in the Eucharist (see Chapter Six and Jn 6).

And most of all, in a paradoxical way, Jesus' passion and death reveal His royal status as the true Davidic king (see Chapter Eight). He is crowned, but with thorns; He is vested with a royal robe, but in mockery; He is hailed as a king by the soldiers, but in jest. His royal elevation is not to a throne but to a cross with a simple sign above His head that reads, "Jesus the Nazorean, King of the Jews." Though the Romans intended all this to mock Jesus' royal claims, the Gospel writers highlight how they unwittingly reveal the truth: Jesus is, in fact, the true King of Kings. While His crucifixion is seen by the world to be His moment of defeat, it is actually His moment of triumph over sin and death. Through the cross, Jesus takes on the cures of Adam and dies for our sins, freeing us from death so that we might share eternal life with him (CCC, 602; Rom 5:12f.; 1 Cor 15:56). His execution, therefore, is really His enthronement as He establishes his kingdom, the Church.

Not Just the Jews

Jesus clearly fulfills all the covenants God made to His people. However, God's people are not just the Jews; like David himself, the messianic son of David is to reign over *all* of Israel, which originally consisted of all twelve tribes. As we saw in the previous chapter, the Jews, as the name suggests, are those Israelites who remained loyal to the divinely established Davidic dynasty in the southern kingdom of Judah. The ten northern tribes rebelled against their king and established their own kingdom, only to be invaded by the Assyrians in 722 B.C.—which became known as Samaria.

The Assyrians had a particular way of treating their vanquished foes. Most of the defeated Israelites were scattered into foreign territories, but a small portion of them were left behind in the land. The Assyrians then brought in pagans from five other nations that they had conquered (2 Kgs 17:24-31). The result was that the northern tribes remaining in the land found themselves dwelling side by side with pagan peoples and their idolatrous practices. They eventually intermarried with these people, yoking themselves to their pagan way of life and even their foreign gods. It was thus that the ten northern tribes lost their ethnic and religious identity.

In Jesus' time, this mixed population of descendants from the old northern kingdom was known collectively as the Samaritans. They were hated by their estranged brethren, the Jews, for their unfaithfulness to God throughout the centuries and for their intermarriage with godless people. In fact, God sent the prophets to the northern kingdom and warned them that their idolatry was an act of covenant infidelity, likening it to adultery. This was a most fitting description, since God's covenant relationship with Israel was likened to the kind of intimate union that exists between a husband and wife: God was the bridegroom and Israel was His bride. The Samaritans' unfaithfulness to the covenant and their worshiping of other gods was, according to the prophets, similar to the infidelity of a spouse.

Yet even in the face of Israel's spiritual adultery, the prophet Hosea tells the people that there will be a time when the Lord, the divine husband, will come to his spouse again, speak to her in love, and call her back into relationship.

> Therefore, behold, I will allure her, and bring her into the wilderness, and speak tenderly to her…. For I will remove the names of the Ba'als from her mouth, and they shall be mentioned by name no more. And I will make for you a covenant…. And I will betroth you to me for ever; I will betroth you to me in righteousness and in justice, in steadfast love, and in mercy. I will betroth you to me in faithfulness; and you shall know the Lord. (Hos 2:14, 17-18, 19-20)

This prophecy was given just before the northern kingdom was conquered by the Assyrians. To give this destitute Samaritan people hope, God reminds them that He will *never* abandon His bride. He foretells that, despite her infidelities, He will speak kindly to her and eventually woo her back into the fullness of His covenant love.

All's Well that Ends Well: John 4

This background provides important context for understanding Jesus' public ministry in the Gospel of John. After gathering Jewish disciples in Galilee (Jn 1) and teaching and performing miracles for the Jews in Jerusalem (Jn 2), Jesus takes His disciples into the land of Judea where they begin to baptize the Jews (Jn 3). John the Baptist sees the call to Christ's baptism as a spousal gesture, referring to Jesus as the bridegroom coming for His chosen people (Jn 3:29-30).

But Jesus' bride is not just the Jews, and the chosen people extend beyond the borders of Judea. Thus, Jesus next leaves

Judea and goes to Samaria, the land where many people from the separated ten northern tribes dwell.

As He enters this region, Jesus goes to a well where a woman comes to draw water—an evocative setting in light of the Old Testament. Many of Israel's ancient leaders found their wives at a well: Isaac's wife Rebecca (Gn 24:11), Jacob's wife Rachel (Gn 29:2), and Moses's wife Zipporah (Ex 2:15). Now, Jesus, who already has been described as the "bridegroom" in John's Gospel, meets a Samaritan woman at a well.

He asks her for a drink, which shocks her. She says, "How is it that you, a Jew, ask a drink of me, a woman of Samaria?" (Jn 4:9). Her surprise reflects the tragic history of her people, who had been at odds with their Jewish kinsmen for nearly a thousand years. Coming as the new, royal son of David, Jesus breaks down these barriers and speaks kindly to this Samaritan woman.

As we listen to their conversation, we discover that the Samaritan woman has had a heart-wrenching life—and one that actually embodies the disastrous history of her nation. She has suffered through the misery of marital infidelity. Like Samaria, she had been an adulterous wife; she had yoked herself to five different men, just as Samaria had yoked itself to five foreign nations and their idolatrous practices (2 Kgs 17:29-34). Her life, therefore, is an icon of the covenant infidelity of Israel that Hosea had condemned.

But now, Jesus tenderly approaches her as the divine bridegroom seeking out unfaithful Samaria to woo her back into covenant union, just as Hosea prophesied. He speaks gently to her and extends His loving mercy. As the ever-faithful husband, Jesus does not reject her but invites her to return to God's kingdom.

At the same time, Jesus reminds her that "salvation is from the Jews" (Jn 4:22). This is a reference to God's plan to save all humanity through the Davidic dynasty—a plan that the Samaritans rejected. The woman now realizes she is standing in the presence of a great prophet and asks Jesus about the Jewish belief in the coming of a savior from the line of David, a messiah-king. Jesus, the true son of David, replies, "I who speak to you am he" (Jn 2:26).

The woman comes to believe in Jesus and tells others of her great discovery. Many Samaritans begin to believe in Christ and thus return to their bridegroom (Jn 4:39-42). In this one scene, God Himself has come to draw this woman—and the estranged Samaritan people whom she represents—back to His heart. And many of the Samaratans in this scene come to recognize that Jesus, the Jewish messiah, is the savior not only of the Jews but of all of Israel, including the Samaritans—no matter how far they have strayed. Indeed they proclaim that Jesus is "Savior of the World" (Jn 4:42).

To All the Nations

This inclusion of the Samaritans is just the first step of extending the Kingdom of David beyond the Jewish people. As Jesus begins to gather the lost sheep of Israel, we are reminded that the promises given to Abraham and David were not just for the twelve tribes of Israel but for the entire human family. We have seen throughout this study that God always intended to use the people of Israel and the kingdom of David as His instruments to gather back all the families of the earth into covenant union.

Thus, Jesus, at the beginning of His public ministry, reminds Israel of its universal mission, summoning the people to be the "light of the world" and the "salt of the earth" (Mt 5:13-14). He Himself consistently welcomes the sinners, covenant outcasts, and gentiles into His kingdom (see Mt 8:1-13, 9:9-13). He even praises the faith of a Roman centurion and the humility of a Syro-Phoenecian woman as more remarkable than the faith He has witnessed in Israel.

Indeed, His final act before ascending into heaven is to remind the Church of its worldwide mission:

> Go therefore and make disciples of all nations, baptizing them in the name of the Father and of the Son and of the Holy Spirit, teaching them to observe all that I have commanded you; and lo, I am with you always, to the close of the age. (Mt 28:19-20)

The Mission of the Church (Acts 1:8)

This mission of Jesus to the Jews, the Samaritans, and the gentiles is continued in the Church. In fact, the Book of Acts reveals the Church's mission as a recapitulation of Christ's public ministry.

The Acts of the Apostles begins with a subtle but important point: "In the first book…I have dealt with all that Jesus began to do and teach" (Acts. 1:1). What is this "first book"? It is the Gospel of Luke, which covers Christ's life from the incarnation to His ascension. Acts 1:1 reminds us, however, that Luke's Gospel is just the start of what Jesus *began* to do and teach. In this second volume, known as the Acts of the Apostles, Luke will focus on what Jesus *continues* to do and teach through His Church. This highlights a fundamental principle: What Jesus did in His physical body two thousand years ago, He continues to do throughout history in His mystical body, the Church.

Just as Jesus had proclaimed His kingdom to Jerusalem, Judea, Samaria, and the gentiles, so now He commands His disciples to do the same. He tells them, "But you shall receive power when the Holy Spirit has come upon you; and you shall be my witnesses in Jerusalem, and in all Judea and Samaria and to the end of the earth" (Acts 1:8).

This single verse serves as a table of contents for the evangelical mission of the early Church as outlined in Acts of the Apostles. The apostles, like their Master, will have the Holy Spirit descend upon them, and then they will preach the kingdom to the Jews. They begin their ministry in Jerusalem at Pentecost, sharing the Gospel of the King with Jews from all over the world (Acts 2). However, after persecution breaks out in Jerusalem, many Christians flee the city, and soon the Gospel spreads to Judea and then to Samaria, as multitudes outside Jerusalem are drawn into the Church (Acts 8).

After the conversion of Paul (Acts 9), he and the other Christian leaders take the Gospel of the Kingdom to the ends of the earth, moving outward through Asia Minor, Greece, and all the way to the heart of Roman Empire, the capital city of Rome itself. By the conclusion of Acts, we are told that Paul is there "preaching the kingdom of God and teaching about the Lord Jesus Christ quite openly and unhindered" (Acts 28:31).

Thus, at the end of Acts, this universal kingdom, which began with the mustard seed of Jesus' life, is now taking root in Rome. Its branches have extended throughout the known world, through the witness of the apostles and those men they appointed to succeed them to gather all nations into the one, holy, catholic, and apostolic Church. Indeed, God's third promise to Abraham for a worldwide family is now being fulfilled through Jesus Christ and the Church He established.

Something Beautiful for God

And the drama of salvation history continues throughout the centuries with men and women from generation to generation coming in and out of the story—some as heroes who give their lives to God, others as mediocre figures who fail to succeed in their role and still others who stubbornly refuse to follow God's ways.

Now you are being invited into this story. You are called to play a part in God's plan of salvation and to help extend His Kingdom on earth. In the words of Mother Teresa, you are called to make your life "something beautiful for God." How well will you play your part in the story? Will you be like Moses, Joshua and Paul who exhibited Christ's sacrificial love and generously used their lives not for their own purposes, but for God's? Or will you be like the people at Babel or at the end of the Book of Judges who opposed God's moral law, set up their own morality and pursued whatever they thought was right in their own eyes? Or will you be like Samson and King Saul who were given many talents to be used for good, but who selfishly used their lives to pursue the glories and pleasures of this world more than the will of God?

The story of salvation history now passes on to you. Many great men and women have gone before you in this drama. How well will you play your part? Will you be the hero of your life? Only the pages of your life will tell.

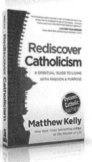

ENDNOTES

[1] "The 'tree of knowledge of good and evil' symbolically evokes the insurmountable limits that man, being a creature, must freely recognize and respect with trust. Man is dependent on his Creator and subject to the laws of creation and to the moral norms that govern the use of freedom" (CCC 396). Man's eventual eating from this tree symbolizes his unwillingness to accept this dependance on God. Man instead uses his freedom to try to establish what is good and evil for himself apart from God. He seeks to "be like God" but without God (CCC, 398). But this leads to tragic consequences for man—separation from God and the introduction of sin and division into the human family. Through the law given in Gn 3:16-17, God wants to protect man from this grave danger.

[2] John Paul II, *Veritatis Splendor*, 35.

[3] Parts of this chapter were based on an article by Edward Sri "From the Father's Heart: God's Law and Our Happiness" *Lay Witness* May/June 2011, pp. 10-11.

[4] N. T. Wright, *Following Jesus* (Grand Rapids: Eerdmans, 1994), p. 23.

[5] St. Augustine, *The City of God* (New York: Penguin Books, 1984), p. 593.

[6] Some have interpreted the "sons of God" as a reference to angelic beings who marry women, but this view seems unlikely.

Apart from the fact that angels cannot reproduce like humans (as St. Augustine and St. Thomas Aquinas have noted), nowhere in Genesis is the notion of "sons of God" associated with angels, and nothing in the immediate context would point us in that direction.

That the "sons of God" should be understood as the faithful Sethite line is made clearer when we consider how Genesis itself links the notion of being a son of God with the genealogy of Adam and Seth. This is the only genealogy in the Old Testament that begins with a reference to God Himself: "When God created man, he made him in the likeness of God" (Gn 5:1). The genealogy then tells how Adam "became the father of a son in his own likeness, after his image, and named him Seth" (Gn 5:3) and then traces the descendants of Seth all the way down to Noah. The parallel between God's creating Adam in His image and likeness (Gn 1:26, 5:3) and Adam fathering Seth "after his image" and "in his own likeness" (Gn 5:3) underscores how God has a special father-son relationship with these faithful descendants of Adam and Seth. As Biblical scholar John Sailhamer put it, "The author has gone to great lengths to depict God's creation of humankind in terms of a patriarch establishing and overseeing a family.... Not only is Adam the father of Seth and Seth the father of Enosh and so on, but God is the father of them all." John H. Sailhamer, *The Pentateuch as Narrative* (Grand Rapids: Zondervan, 1990), p. 117.

[7] The prohibition against "looking upon your father's nakedness" becomes even clearer when we consider that it is given as a

warning to the Israelites before entering the Promised Land, which is the land of Canaan, inhabited by the descendants of the disgraced son of Ham (see Lv 18:3).

[8] John Bergsma and Scott Hahn, "Noah's Nakedness and the Curse on Canaan (Genesis 9:20-27)," *Journal of Biblical Literature* 124.1 (Spring 2005), pp. 25-40.

[9] "Hymn to the Nile" in ANET, 372-3. See Goran Larson, *Bound for Freedom* (Peabody, Massachusetts: Hendrickson, 1999), p. 60. On the plagues and Egyptian idolatry, see also John J. Davis, *Moses and the gods of Egypt*, 2nd ed. (Winona Lake, Indiana: BMH Books, 1998).

[10] Scott Hahn, *A Father Who Keeps His Promises* (Ann Arbor: Servant, 1995), pp. 136-39.

[11] Christopher J. H. Wright, *Knowing Jesus Through the Old Testament* (Downers Grove, Illinois: IVP Academic, 1995).

[12] We are thankful to Curtis Mitch for this insight.

[13] The firstborn were counted at 22,273 men, giving 273 more firstborn than Levites (Nm 3:40). In order to account for the excess of 273 firstborn, these were ransomed back at a price of five shekels a piece so that there would be a perfectly even exchange (Nm 3:46-47).

[14] Christopher J. H. Wright, *Deuteronomy* (Grand Rapids: Baker, 1994).

[15] Victor P. Hamilton, *Handbook on the Historical Books* (Grand Rapids: Baker), p.153.

[16] Scott Hahn, *Kinship by Covenant* (Ann Arbor: UMI Dissertation Services, 1995), p. 320.

[17] See the translation and explanation in Scott Hahn, *Kinship by Covenant* (Ann Arbor: UMI Dissertation Services, 1995), pp. 322, 346-7. See also Scott Hahn, *A Father Who Keeps His Promises* (Cincinnati: Servant Books, 1998), p. 213.

[18] When read in the context of all of Scripture, this figure points to the demonic beast in the Book of Revelation, whose number is 666. In fact, it is the only other passage in the Bible where this number is used.

KEY TO BIBLICAL ABBREVIATIONS

The following abbreviations are used for the various Scriptural verses cited throughout the book. (*Note: CCC = Catechism of the Catholic Church.*)

OLD TESTAMENT

Gn	Genesis	Tb	Tobit	Ez	Ezekiel
Ex	Exodus	Jdt	Judith	Dn	Daniel
Lv	Leviticus	Est	Esther	Hos	Hosea
Nm	Numbers	1 Mc	1 Maccabees	Jl	Joel
Dt	Deuteronomy	2 Mc	2 Maccabees	Am	Amos
Jos	Joshua	Jb	Job	Ob	Obadiah
Jgs	Judges	Ps	Psalms	Jon	Jonah
Ru	Ruth	Prv	Proverbs	Mi	Micah
1 Sam	1 Samuel	Eccl	Ecclesiastes	Na	Nahum
2 Sam	2 Samuel	Sng	Song of Songs	Hb	Habakkuk
1 Kgs	1 Kings	Wis	Wisdom	Zep	Zephaniah
2 Kgs	2 Kings	Sir	Sirach	Hg	Haggai
1Chr	1 Chronicles	Is	Isaiah	Zec	Zechariah
2 Chr	2 Chronicles	Jer	Jeremiah	Mal	Malachi
Ezr	Ezra	Lam	Lamentations		
Neh	Nehemiah	Bar	Baruch		

NEW TESTAMENT

Mt	Matthew	Phil	Philippians	Jas	James
Mk	Mark	Col	Colossians	1 Pt	1 Peter
Lk	Luke	1 Thess	1Thessalonians	2 Pt	2 Peter
Jn	John	2 Thess	2 Thessalonians	1 Jn	1 John
Acts	Acts	1 Tm	1 Timothy	2 Jn	2 John
Rom	Romans	2 Tm	2 Timothy	3 Jn	3 John
1 Cor	1 Corinthians	Ti	Titus	Jude	Jude
Gal	Galatians	Phlm	Philemon	Rv	Revelation
Eph	Ephesians	Heb	Hebrews		

Curtis Martin is the President and Founder of FOCUS, the Fellowship of Catholic University Students, one of the fastest growing movements in the Catholic Church. In reflecting on the work of FOCUS, Cardinal Timothy Dolan stated, "If you're looking for hope, look to FOCUS."

Whether he is on college campuses or television, at conferences or working with corporate America, Curtis is an award-winning and proven dynamic speaker who has the ability to help his audience discover a vision for life. Through humor, stories, and his own captivating life experiences, Curtis allows people to see how faith in God is lived out in everyday life. He equips people with the tools to discover the fullness of life and happiness beyond imagination.

Curtis Martin holds a Masters degree in Theology and is the author of the best-selling book *Made for More*, co-author of *Boys to Men: The Transforming Power of Virtue and Family Matters: A Scripture Study on Marriage and Family* and co-host the new ground-breaking show on EWTN, *Crossing the Goal*. In 2004, Curtis and his wife Michaelann were awarded the Benemerenti Medal by Pope John Paul II for their outstanding service to the Church. He was awarded the 2006 John Lancaster Spalding Award from the Diocese of Peoria and the 2007 Outstanding Catholic Leadership Award given by the Catholic Leadership Institute In 2011, Pope Benedict XVI appointed Curtis as a Consulter to the Pontifical Council of the New Evangelization. In addition to his work with FOCUS, Curtis serves as the Vice Chairman of the Augustine Institute in Denver, a Catholic graduate school dedicated to the New Evangelization. Curtis and his wife, Michaelann, live in Westminster, CO with five of their eight children.

For more information on Curtis Martin please visit:
http://www.focus.org/about/curtis-martin.html

Dr. Edward (Ted) Sri is a nationally-known Catholic speaker who appears regularly on EWTN. He is the author of several best-selling books, including *A Biblical Walk through the Mass: Understanding What We Say and Do in the Liturgy* (Ascension press); *The New Rosary in Scripture: Biblical Insights for Praying the 20 Mysteries* (Servant) and *Men, Women and the Mystery of Love: Practical Insights on John Paul II's Love and Responsibility* (Servant).

Edward is a founding leader with Curtis Martin of FOCUS (Fellowship of Catholic University Students) and the general editor of *Symbolon RCIA* and *Opening the Word*, a journey through the Sunday Mass Readings. He currently serves as Vice President of Mission and Outreach and professor of theology and Scripture at the Augustine Institute Master's program in Denver, Colorado. He also leads multiple pilgrimages to Rome for parishes, groups and lay people each year. Edward holds a doctorate from the Pontifical University of St. Thomas Aquinas in Rome. He resides with his wife Elizabeth and their six children in Littleton, Colorado.

Other books by Edward Sri include: *The Bible Compass: A Catholic's Guide to Navigating the Scriptures* (Ascension Press); *Mystery of the Kingdom: On the Gospel of Matthew* (Emmaus Road), *Queen Mother: A Biblical Theology of Mary's Queenship* (Emmaus Road); *Dawn of the Messiah: The Coming of Christ in Scripture* (Servant) and *The Da Vinci Deception: 100 Questions About the Facts and Fiction of The Da Vinci Code* (Ascension Press) (coauthored with Mark Shea); *The Gospel of Matthew* (Baker Academic). He also is a contributor to the popular apologetics series, *Catholic for a Reason* and a recent volume on Catholic Marian theology called *Mariology* (Queenship Publishing).

Dr. Edward Sri is a sought out Catholic speaker on a wide variety of topics. To schedule Dr. Edward Sri for a presentation or talk for a parish, diocese or other large group event, please contact Dr. Sri at info@augustineinstitute.org.